OPEN
HOUSE

SHERIDAN VOYSEY IN CONVERSATION WITH TIM COSTELLO, ANDREW DENTON, CLIVE HAMILTON, THOMAS KENEALLY, MAX LUCADO, PHILIP YANCEY AND MANY MORE.

Hope you enjoy this!

STRAND PUBLISHING
Sydney

Open House
Copyright © 2008 Sheridan Voysey/Christian Broadcasting Association Ltd
First published 2007 by Strand Publishing

The Open House radio program is a production of Sydney's 103.2: www.fm1032.com.au

ISBN 978–1-921202–49–0

Distributed in Australia by:
Family Reading Publications
B100 Ring Road
Ballarat Victoria 3350
Phone: (03) 5334 3244
Fax: (03) 5334 3299
Email: sales@familyreading.com.au
Web: www.familyreading.com.au

The words of Jesus Christ on page 1 are taken from John 10:10, *The Holy Bible, New International Version®*. Copyright © 1973, 1978, 1984 by the International Bible Society. Used by permission of Zondervan Publishing House.
The words of Saint Paul on page 83 are taken from Romans 12:1, *The Message* paraphrase of the Bible by Eugene H. Peterson. Copyright © 1993, 1994, 1995, 1996, 2000. Used by permission of NavPress Publishing Group. All rights reserved.
The words of King David on page 193 are taken from Psalm 24:1, *The Holy Bible, New International Version*.

Edited by Owen Salter
Cover design by Joy Lankshear
Typeset by Midland Typesetters, Australia
Printed by Griffin Press

Contents

Contents

Culture:

Introduction

Every Sunday evening a unique conversation takes place; a gathering of people from different backgrounds, with varied viewpoints, who come to explore life's questions and share life's lessons. That conversation is a national talkback radio program called Open House, and it is my privilege to host it.

Each week Open House is visited by some wonderful guests; a variety of authors, artists and activists ready to talk about life, faith and culture. The laughter, tears and wisdom in these conversations is too good to air just once, so we've brought you some of the 'best' interviews so far in the pages that follow.

If the Chinese proverb is true and a single conversation with a wise person is worth a month's study of books, then this collection of interviews could be the equivalent of a Masters course in life, with topics ranging from God, pain, success and poverty to masculinity, materialism, politics and art. Max Lucado will help you find your calling in life; you'll discover the people and experiences that shaped Tony Campolo; Philip Yancey will let you into his writing secrets; and Alister McGrath will give you his response to *The God Delusion*. You'll smile at Adrian Plass's description of church life, cry with John Smith as he fears never seeing his children again, and be struck by the gravity of Tim Flannery's ecological predictions. You'll marvel at Terry Waite's endurance through captivity, ponder the emptiness that once plagued Marina Prior's soul, and throughout the book, hear how people with faith and tenacity are leaving an indelible mark on this world.

So far, Open House has been served by two brilliant producers: Katrina Roe and Kirsty Lee. I thank them both for their invaluable role in crafting a credible, entertaining program. Kirsty's background research for the John Anderson, Jeffrey Sachs, Terry Waite, Duncan Armstrong, Katherine Paterson, Thomas Keneally and Adrian Plass interviews is especially noted. Apart from some cosmetic editing for flow or brevity, these transcripts are presented as they aired. In some cases material that was edited from the audio interview has been included here.

As a radio program, Open House explores life, faith and culture from a Christian perspective. Many featured in these pages share that faith, and some do not. Irrespective of their backgrounds, through these guests I have learnt much about the complexities of life and the contemporary search for belief.

I believe you will too.

Sheridan Voysey

LIFE

Modern man has both feet firmly planted in mid-air.
Francis Schaeffer

I have come that they may have life, and have it to the full.
Jesus Christ

Terry Waite

YOU CAN BREAK MY BODY, BEND MY MIND, BUT MY SOUL IS
NOT YOURS TO POSSESS

In 1987 Terry Waite travelled to Lebanon on a mission to free hostages. Through a contact's betrayal, Terry himself was taken hostage and held in solitary confinement for nearly five years. While his family agonised, Terry received what news he could through fellow hostages tapping in code through his cell wall.

Terry's release from his Islamic Jihad captors made international news in 1991. How did he survive the mental torment of solitary confinement? What resources did his faith provide during the ordeal? Who has he become in the years since? Those are some of the questions I to put to Terry, and the unfolding story proved riveting.

Describe that day in 1987 when you, as the Church of England's envoy, were taken hostage. It must be indelibly locked in your mind.
I remember the day very well. I went back into Beirut at a time of extreme difficulty. I still remember that I thought my chances of being captured, or even being killed, were very high. But I went back for very clear reasons. I had been a victim of political duplicity and I wasn't going to fall victim to that, if I could help it, any further. Secondly, the hostages that I knew were extremely distressed and I felt that there was just a chance that something might be done.

3

I went back. I was promised safe conduct by the captors of the hostages and they broke their promise. I spent about four-and-a-half years in solitary confinement and another six months in the company of other hostages.

Describe that sense of betrayal by your captors.
At the time I was very angry. When I found myself in an underground tiled cell, I really was angry with them for breaking their word, and I did what many prisoners do when they are first incarcerated—demonstrate that I still had a measure of freedom. So I refused all food for a week. At the end of the first week they said that if I didn't eat they'd make me eat. So I ate. My anger had dissipated. I think anger is a normal human emotion; we all have it. It is important to be able to control it, obviously, but it is even more important not to allow it to turn into bitterness, because bitterness is like a cancer that enters the soul—it does more harm to those who hold it than against those whom it is held.

As the years go by I can understand why my kidnappers behaved as they did. I don't agree with it. I don't agree with kidnapping, with taking innocent people. But I can see that when some people have always been at the bottom of the heap politically, economically and socially, when they have always been pushed against the wall, when they have been ignored, when they have seen nothing but warfare, when they feel that they have been totally exploited, I can see why they turn to desperate measures.

And that leads me to say something about the way in which we deal with so-called terrorism today. Terrorism, including kidnapping and all those sort of things, is really a symptom of a much deeper disorder. The more I think about it the more I am able to recognise that these are symptoms, and we have to deal with the fundamental problems rather than just dealing with the symptoms.

How long did you initially think you would be held for?
Like most people who are captured, you feel as though this will be over in twenty-four hours. When twenty-four hours have passed you say, well, it can't be longer than a few days. Then the first week goes by, then a month, then two months, six months and then twelve months go by. In my case I had interrogation for the first year; they were trying to see if I knew anything about what became the Iran-Contra affair. Mercifully I knew nothing about that, and at the end of the first year they were convinced I had been a victim of political duplicities and they were going to release me. They put me in good accommodation for a week and then some event took place, I wasn't released, and I went back into normal hostage accommodation.

Again I thought, well, it won't be long. But it just goes on and on. After that you learn to live a day at a time, and you never believe anything until it has actually happened. I was told several times that I'd be released in the next few days, but then the days would go by. So you live each day as it comes.

Tell us about that political duplicity briefly, just so we can get the context of the story.
In working for hostage release, my way was to have face-to-face contact with hostage takers. For example, I was effective in bringing the release of hostages in Iran at the time of the Iranian revolution. I had face-to-face encounters with Colonel Gaddafi and was able to bring people home from Libya. Years before, when I was a comparatively young man, I had face-to-face dealings with the 'last

king of Scotland', Idi Amin in Uganda. So I had met a varied group of characters.

My way of dealing has always been a face-to-face encounter, try and build up a relationship of trust and try and get to the underlying issues. I want to find out why they're behaving the way they are and then try and find a way of resolving the problem without violence, or without breaking the law, or without payment.

In Lebanon I had a relationship with the captors and was meeting with them on a fairly regular basis. Unfortunately, the American administration had another line altogether and they went to Iran, who at the time were fighting the Iran/Iraq war. The Americans went to Iran and said that if Iran would pressure their clients Hezbollah in Lebanon—Hezbollah were the group who were keeping me, eventually—and pressure them to release hostages, then they would give them arms to fight the war against Iraq. Iran agreed to that, arms were delivered, slight pressure was applied, one hostage was released, and that I think came as a major surprise to Hezbollah. Then Hezbollah said, well, Terry Waite knows the Americans. Let's take him and see what he knows about this deal. That was why I was captured and that was the whole essence of my interrogation. That's what I mean by falling victim to political duplicity.

So here you are in solitary confinement for nearly five years. How on earth do you cope for that amount of time?
It's an extreme situation. It can be depressing, because you see your skin go white because you have no natural light. You lose muscle tone because there is no exercise other than what you can do on the end of a chain—you were chained twenty-four hours a day to the wall. You're sitting on the floor in a dark room with no books and papers for a long, long time and no communication with

anyone or with the outside world. I remember seeing my beard grow long and turning white; it had been black. I felt I was getting old before my time.

When you see your physical body beginning to deteriorate, you have to learn to live within. You become afraid that you might also deteriorate rather more quickly than you would want to, both mentally and spiritually.

Your mind must start to play games on you.
Yes, indeed. And you have got to be able to discipline your mind, because everything is lived from within. There is no external stimulation. There is no books, no one to speak with, no one to feed your identity back to you.

I was fortunate, firstly, because through life I had been an avid reader and therefore I had built up a store of books, poetry and prose in my memory. Secondly, I'd been brought up as an Anglican—I'm an Anglican Christian—and had been brought up with the Book of Common Prayer. The language of that was very, very helpful. I had unconsciously memorised it as a choir boy. If I can just give you an example of what I mean from one of the great old collects of the prayer book:

> Lighten our darkness, we beseech thee, O Lord; and by
> thy great mercy defend us from all perils and dangers
> of this night . . .

That is very, very meaningful when you're sitting in darkness. That collect not only has meaning but it also has poetry and rhythm. There is a relationship between identity, language and prayer; somehow they help you hold together at your centre.

Some people may find this strange, but I never engaged in what is called extemporary prayer during that time. I felt that if I did I would be begin to, sort of, go down a one-way track, reveal my own psychological vulnerability and just get into the business of saying, 'Oh God, get me out of here'—which isn't prayer at all. That's just being like a child. So by falling back on that which I knew, the Prayer Book and the balance of that, I was able to keep a bit more balance in my mind and also maintain some degree of inner balance.

Wasn't there a time, though, when you did just want to cry out and say, 'God, save me!'?
Oh yes, there was, there was. But, you know, I'm a believer in this: if you put yourself in dangerous situations, as I did—no one forced me to go, it was my choice—and if things go wrong, you take responsibility. You don't blame other people and you certainly can't blame God! You expect that you will be supported, and I was supported. But you have to work for that support; it isn't just a question of it falling down from heaven and landing on your head.

There is something in the Bible that talks about being a co-creator with God, and that involves tremendous responsibility. If you are a co-creator then you've got to be responsible for your own development, just as you have to be responsible for development of the environment and relationships with your neighbours and so on. You've got a real responsibility; you must live up to it. So don't try and palm it off on God or somebody else.

Terry, I don't want to leave the whole question of faith yet, because I think it's a fascinating aspect of your story. You said you weren't blaming

God, but was there ever a moment when you felt your faith challenged? Often that's when our faith is really put to the test.

I have to say I never felt that. What I did feel was this: religion is a remarkable phenomenon because it attracts all sorts of encumbrances around it, many of which are just sheer nonsense in my view. But when you are out on a limb, when you are at the extremities, somehow you try and get to the real heart of the matter, try and cut through the nonsense and get to the real essence of belief and being.

If I can put it very, very simply—and this may seem too simple for some—I could say this in the face of my captors: you have the power to break my body, and you have tried; you have the power to bend my mind, and you have tried; but my soul is not yours to possess. There was that essential belief that my soul lay in the hands of God and couldn't be taken by others.

Now, we can argue till the cows come home, as people have done across the generations, about what the soul is. For me it is the sum-total of *me*—my identity, my essential being, which lay in the hands of God and couldn't be taken by others. And that very, very simple belief was enough to enable me to retain hope.

If anybody listening to this is in a situation of real unpleasantness, difficulty, sickness or whatever, realise that you are not going to be destroyed. If you face suffering it will be very difficult; there may be no relief from the suffering. But if you can have hope behind it you will not be destroyed.

During your captivity what is your family going through? I believe they didn't even know whether you were alive or dead.

Someone who came back from Beirut or came out of Beirut, I don't quite know what, told my wife, 'Your husband is dead.' She asked how they knew and they said, 'We've seen his grave.' She said, 'Well, I'll believe it when I see it.' She never believed that I was dead, and the family held on.

I have great admiration for my wife. We have four children, grown up now, and grandchildren. She had to keep the children and the family together and see them through school and halfway through university. It was very difficult for them. In some ways it is more difficult for families than it is for the hostage, because they just don't know, and they go on not knowing, and have to live normal life with all the pressures.

But we came through it and I think in fact it has done us good. It sounds absolutely silly to say that. Perhaps a better way to put it is that we've refused to allow it to do us harm. Again, I think this is the business of taking events as far as you can in your own hands. I said a moment ago that suffering is always difficult, and it is. I'm the last one to underplay it and the last one to treat it lightly. But it needn't destroy. Very often it can be turned around so that you can make something creative of it. If you look back into history you will find that many great acts of creativity came out of suffering. And, of course, the central symbol of the Christian faith is a symbol of suffering—the cross. But beyond that lies the symbol of hope—the resurrection.

I can't imagine the feelings that must've been flowing through you when you saw your wife and kids for the first time after five years of solitary confinement.
I didn't know my son. I mean, my son was a young lad when I was taken and he was now a mature teenager. He's now a school master actually; he's head of sixth form these days with children of his own. But I wouldn't have recognised him.

It took time. It took time to get together again. If anybody is listening to this who has been through a long period of separation or trauma, don't imagine that you are going to rush back and everything is going to be wonderful. It may be, and that would be fortunate. But take time. Someone said to me, 'When you come out after an experience like that, take it as though you are coming up from the sea bed. If you come up too quickly you get the bends; if you take it gently you will be fine.' That was good advice.

How were you finally released? What was the turning point?
Simply the end of the political saga in the Middle East. They simply came into the room, gave me some clothes which didn't fit—I'm six foot seven—so, you know, I looked like I was wearing Boy Scout trousers . . .

Ready for the cameras rolling as you leave . . .
They probably said, 'There's Waite again, looking elegant as usual!'
[Laughter]
I looked like a scarecrow. I looked dreadful.

I bet your kids were saying, 'Oh Dad, come on!'
Yeah, 'Come on, get yourself a suit.' Well, what do you mean? This is my best suit! In Australia they all dress like this!
[Laughter]

Let's talk about the Terry Waite of today. You've founded a group called Hostage UK to support families who experience what you and your family experienced.
I'd been working as an envoy for the Archbishop of Canterbury and I had had a salaried job. When I came out of captivity I thought,

I'm not going to go back into a salaried job. What I am going to do is earn my own living by writing and lecturing, and then give the rest of the time away. I wouldn't have had the courage to do that before the captivity. You become dependent on a monthly salary. But I thought, I can manage this. I've faced that sort of a risk, I can face this one. And Hostage UK is one of the organisations I founded.

How many hostages are taken around the world each year?
I don't know how many but it's an enormous number, it really is. Often families are bewildered, wondering how to behave, what to do, how far to trust the Government, what provisions should be made, should we go out there, etc. There's nothing like someone who has been through the experience, either as a family member or as a hostage themselves, being able to go and sit with a family and really relate to the real issues that they face.

You may have heard of the hostage Ken Bigly, who was one of those brutally beheaded in Iraq. I went and sat with his mother, an old lady in Liverpool. I sat on the end of her bed. She was in her eighties, the news had come through that Ken, her son, had been beheaded, and she said to me, 'There is nothing that can describe how I feel as a mother at this time.' Then she went on, 'But my suffering is no greater than the suffering of a mother in Iraq who has just lost her child.' I thought, how remarkable. That lady is going through all that at this moment and is able to extend her compassion to someone whom she has never met. It was a remarkable thing to be able to say.

A very gracious statement. As you sit with these people, doesn't it bring back the memories for you?
There are memories and there are memories, but you have to come

to terms with them. We were fortunate that when I came out of captivity we were able to talk about the experience. That is part of the answer. If when you have been through a trauma you are able to objectify it, either by talking about it with someone who is a good listener, probably a professional, or through writing about the experience, you can manage it. If you push it deep down inside yourself, the chances are that it will resurrect many years later and manage you negatively.

Another thing I do is work with far eastern prisoners of war—former prisoners of the Japanese. When those fellows came out of the Japanese camps they were given a few shillings in England and told to get on with it. And, interestingly enough, they were told not to speak about the experience. I've listened to so many of them, and I've listened to their children and their wives, and they say that in their sixties they began having flashbacks and all sorts of problems. So, as I say, it is very important that when people go through trauma that help is available.

Wrapping up, what have you learned through your ordeal? What are the great life lessons you've taken out of your hostage experience?
Some people have said that I was a fool to trust people so much. Well, I trusted in a number of instances and the result was that innocent people came home. I trusted in this instance in Beirut and I was captured. There are no guarantees. But I'd rather have a trusting nature than be suspicious of everybody. That doesn't mean that you're naïve, but I think it's better to have a trusting nature than to be closed up and think everybody's against you. That is one thing.

Secondly, suffering needn't destroy. I believe that very, very implicitly.

Thirdly, keep a few simple goals in life and don't be deterred when things go wrong. Things will go wrong. You can't, and shouldn't, have it all your own way. But don't be deterred. Keep going.

And as for questions of faith, which I think are important—when you are at the extremities it is quite simple: don't expect God to get you out of a hole in the way that you expect. But if you have faith you will not be destroyed and you will find that you can live in hope, not just for this life but for dimensions that lie way beyond this life.

John Anderson

Former Prime Minister John Howard once said there was no finer human being in Australian politics than John Anderson. Esteemed by both sides of parliament as the 'Mr Clean' of political life, John Anderson's twenty year parliamentary career saw him rise to become Leader of the National Party and Deputy Prime Minister of Australia.

In 2005 John Anderson stood down as Deputy Prime Minister for health and family reasons, and when he joined us on Open House in August 2007 he was only months away from relinquishing his long-held seat of Gwydir. His insights into political life and his passionate views on faith and public values will not be soon forgotten.

It's been a couple of years since you relinquished the role of Deputy Prime Minister for health reasons, and also to spend more time with your family. Is life any slower for you?
Well, the answer is yes, it is. I suspect that very few people have any real insight into how busy a Federal political leader's life actually is. The hours are extraordinary. The pressure is extraordinary. I'm still busy, but nothing like I was in those days.

Give us a picture of what your average day used to be like.
It depended very much on whether I was in Canberra or out

somewhere in the electorate. As Deputy Prime Minister I suppose I saw the whole of Australia as my electorate.

In Canberra I would typically be in the office by about 7.30 in the morning, having already tried to catch up on some of the news of the day. I'd have any early staff meetings planned; sometimes these were breakfasts so you'd be in even earlier—this dreadful American habit of having no time in the rest of the day so you have breakfast meetings as well. Then the meetings would start around 8.00 am with my chiefs of staff and senior advisors. Then we would have our leadership meeting at 8.30 where the leadership of the coalition—the Prime Minister, the Deputy Prime Minister, the Treasurer and so forth—would meet.

During the morning you might have anything from legislation to introduce through to delegations to see. There were always delegations—always people with genuine reasons who needed to see you. And you were never able, ever, to meet the demand from people who had some particular cause that they wanted to see you about.

Nearly always there would be some function at lunch. If there wasn't, you still wouldn't stop for lunch—you would try and catch up with your paperwork. And you'd never beat the paperwork either. There was always media to do, and then of course at about one o'clock you'd have to prepare for question time, between 2.00 and 3.00 pm.

I usually took further delegations between 3.00 pm and dinner at 6.30. Probably one night out of two there would be some official function at night. Then after dinner we would turn our minds to departmental business, whatever the portfolio issues at the time were.

The problem at that level of politics is that you never know when the next landmine is going to go off—some urgent matter that's totally unforeseeable appearing out of the blue. It might be something 'minor' like a failure in a power supply at a major airport which could have major ramifications, right through to the ultimate one which was the totally unexpected events of September 11.

You can see why you wanted more time with the family too. I'm sure they hardly saw you over those years.
We worked very hard at it. Sunday was always our day. The old saying that on your death bed you're not going to wish you spent more time at the office is absolutely right. But the big issue for me was to make certain that when I was with the family I wasn't giving them second-hand time, through exhaustion or having my mind elsewhere. I was very conscious that I didn't have many years with my children and so I tried to give them what time I could. And of course it's very important to keep a marriage fresh as well.

So it's a very demanding role. And in the end for me, for several years, I had a bit of a health issue which was totally benign, totally non-threatening, but the medical advice was that my lifestyle, the stress levels and the travel was causing it. It manifested itself in interrupted sleep, and in the end it beat me. I was fortunate in a way that it was something that could be managed and now, whilst I wouldn't say it has left me completely, it doesn't really interrupt my life much.

Do you ever miss the rush of politics and the kind of day that you just described?
The answer is no.

There are times when I do wish I was still more central to some of the debates that do interest me—like water and these welfare reforms.

People have focused quite heavily on what the government is doing in the Northern Territory without perhaps realising that it comes with some further welfare reforms which are really needed in electorates like mine, whereby if families on welfare payments are not ensuring that their children are properly clothed, fed and so forth, real action can be taken. The welfare payments won't be denied them; they won't lose any money. But it will be possible if—in the view of the agencies dealing with families and particularly children—the parents' priority expenditure is not to ensure that their kids are clothed, housed, fed and sent to school on time, that from July [2008] that money will be paid into what amounts to a trust account for them. And they will be able to withdraw against it for things like vouchers for the things they should be spending their money on. Money for discretionary expenditure will only be made available to them when they've met their priorities.

That is a very important reform. But it's not just Northern Territory children who are suffering because their parents are abusive or neglectful or have very bad priorities.

Was there any one thing that you didn't get to do before you relinquished the Deputy PM role that you would like to have done?
Many, and that's life. You have to accept that somebody else can take them on. I regret that although I was the architect of what is known as the National Water Initiative, the blueprint for managing Australia's water, the subsequent mechanisms that we have seen so much fighting over—control of the Murray Darling Basin, money and so forth—that I wasn't able to take that further. I think over time I have genuinely taken the view that I've brought it this far, now there are others who can complete it and probably do it better than me.

The welfare reforms which I just outlined: I felt for so long that they were *so* needed but couldn't find a way to get them up. Now they've been done, so I think that's fantastic. So those are just two areas.

But you know I was there for a long time; I was able to do a lot of things and was able to participate in a lot of important debates. I was on the committee, for example, that did the first four budgets when we got into government in 1996. It was very grinding work. There were only a small number of us—the Treasurer, the then Finance Minister, and a few others. That put the nation's budgets back into order, saving nearly $9 billion a year now in interest. Taxpayer's money was going just to service the debt. That's money now that can go into other things, whether it's tax cuts or more overseas aid . . . That's an area where I think, frankly, we should be more engaged in this country. I wish I'd done more in that area.

While you have walked Canberra's corridors of power, you're also a man acquainted with grief. You lost you mother at an early age. You lost your sister to a freak backyard accident. You even lost your son at the age of six months. How have those experiences made you the man you are today?
[Pause]

I don't know that I can entirely answer that.

I'm actually a fairly private person, and I think that had I known that those things were to become known in the public arena and that to some extent people would always come back to them . . . A journalist I respect in Canberra once said, 'John Anderson always seems to return to these subjects.' That is not right. The media always returns to them. Once it became known, after I'd been in public life for probably a decade, that my sister had died in a tragic family accident, the media never left it alone. Indeed, when people sort of look at my life and write about it or whatever, they tend to define me or to some extent paint those things as major influences in my life. Look, I suppose they have been. I don't know that I'm the best judge of *how* influential they've been. I don't know that that is something I'm terribly good at, or whether it's not better to simply leave it to others.

There is no doubt that my sister's death when we were teenagers, which was a truly tragic thing, certainly left me grown up beyond my years, lacking in confidence, and looking for some answers to life. That much I can say.

You write about it in your biography, Faith and Duty, *where you talk about the fact that it was during a cricket game and a simple return of a cricket ball that hit your sister in just the wrong place.*
Yep.

And that actually spurred you on to search for faith, is that right?
I think, looking back on it . . . Just to correct something you said there, I didn't write about it, it was written up by my biographer.

I take it, though, that you were OK with it being included?
Well, he asked questions and I answered them as honestly as I could.

I think it was certainly a catalyst for me. I think the result of that was a fairly chronic loss of confidence in me as a teenager. I felt that anything I hit out firmly against might result in a disaster, you see. It certainly caused me to question very deeply.

How did you regain your confidence?
I don't know that I ever have!

Is that right?
Well, I think it's a hard question and a very personal one in a way. I think what happened after I became a believer, I learnt to put self aside a little bit and tried, to some extent—and I don't want to over-paint this—to learn to say, well, I will simply give things my best shot and not get too worried about whether they work out or not. I will trust God for those things, for the outcomes. That's what I have tried to do.

What was the final turning point for you when it came to Christian belief?
University. At school I had sort of become convinced, I guess at the level of the emotions, that God was real. But it was at university when I was studying European history, which is really the story of our own culture over the last couple of hundred years. The more I looked at it the more I recognised the truth of the biblical assertion that we actually don't want to know God, we'd rather do it our own way, and that the story of the last couple of hundred years is us as a culture finding every excuse, every reason, every rationale we can for rejecting the traditional Christian view of man and this world.

The more I looked at it the more I thought that every attempt to do this has been an unmitigated disaster. And the ultimate disaster was Fascism, which was really about the rejection of any higher authority. It was saying, there is no God, we're not accountable to anybody else, and the only morality is a struggle for power. I thought that if this is where you logically end up when you've rejected the traditional Christian view and you've tried all the other 'isms'—humanism, socialism, communism, whateverism—I thought, I can't go there. For me it just affirmed, at a very deep level, that the truth must lie back where so many of our forefathers believed that it was.

We've got this spate of atheistic books at the moment. In some ways I quite welcome it. It's good to have a debate about these things and I note that these books are selling well. Some of your listeners might have read them.

We've talked about them a lot on Open House.
Well, let me just throw out a couple of questions. This idea from Christopher Hitchens' book that *God is Not Great*. Really? Let's have a look. We gave secularism and atheism a great run in the twentieth century, didn't we? And we had Pol Pot and we had the killing fields and we had the Gulags. Atheistic communism ruined Russia; absolutely ruined it. You had atheism in the form of Fascism. So, the alternative is great? No God is great? Really?

Then look at the other side of the equation and look at the influence of people who took their faith seriously. We have the film *Amazing Grace* around at the moment. Two hundred years ago it was still legal for people in our culture to own other human beings as slaves, and to trade in them. It didn't matter if they died and it didn't matter if you abused them to the point where they collapsed in agony and gave up their spirits. I mean, the treatment was brutal; they were seen as sub-human. Who turned all that around? The great Christian reformers did.

So let's get real about history. I have a love of history. Let's get real about it. What it shows at every point, properly understood, is that the biblical account of man and his condition and the world we live in is the only credible one. That's the point when I realised that I couldn't accept the alternatives.

C.S. Lewis wrote that in 1928 he was the most reluctant

convert in all Christendom. Well, that was only until 1978 when I think I was even more dejected! Because I thought, this is going to be no good; I'll lose all my chances of success and friends. But I believe that it's the truth and I can't walk away from it. And I am more convinced than ever. I am absolutely certain of the truth.

John, has your faith in any way been detrimental to you? Have you lost anything as a result of being a believer in the political realm?
I don't believe so. I don't say that everybody likes it or approves of it. I've certainly been scorned by a couple of the radio shock jocks over time. But, generally speaking, no. I think part of the reason for that is . . . can I say this: my guess is that, despite the too clever by half and very arrogant writings that we were just referring to, this is not going to be an age of irreligion. I think even in Western culture people are beginning to say, well, I don't know whether I can re-embrace it but I'm not too sure where we're going at the moment. That's just in Western culture. The truth is global, of course. This will not be a century of irreligion. This will be a century of great debate and ferment about what we believe, about what stacks up and what doesn't, and there will of course—there already is—be real tensions between opposing views.

The other thing we lose sight of in Australia is this happy materialism that we all blunder along in. We don't need God any more; that it's irrelevant and what have you. But globally this is not a secular age; you've got an explosion of beliefs, and that includes Christianity. Look at China, look at Korea, look at the African continent, look at other parts of Asia, look at South America.

Absolutely. You see faith and searches for faith all around us. There's a whole marketplace of spiritual ideas that people are exploring and the Christian faith is growing right in there. Has your faith changed at all from those early years of belief?

Probably. Not in terms of my core beliefs but in terms of the maturing that, I hope, has taken place. I think it's broadened to an awareness that there are people of real faith in all denominations, and people of no faith who appear to be outwardly faithful in all denominations.

I suppose if I were to wear a label, and I hate labels, but if I were to wear one I suppose I would be seen as a Sydney evangelical [Anglican]. And yet some of the most marvellous Christian friends that I have are from the Catholic tradition, and some of the people who are most difficult and pompous and I think farthest removed from the true humility that is a mark of Christ are some of my fellow travellers in my own denomination.

One of the privileges of this position is that you get to meet people from all around the world. Meeting Christians from the Middle East, for example—there would've been a time when some of the outward manifestations of their faith would have made me choke on my Weet-Bix. But I have matured to the point where I can see now the real depth of conviction in some of them, and I'm very thankful for that. So I think what I have learnt is not to stand on my own pride so much.

What does the future hold for John Anderson? What are the dreams and plans? You're still the member for Gwydir . . .

But only till the next election.

That's for sure?

Absolutely. In political terms, as Newton said towards the end of his lifetime, 'I'm packaged, sealed and waiting for the post.' It's time for me to move on.

My wife and I want to spend more time together. We have a very wonderful marriage. We have four children who are growing up and we want to spend more time with them. We have our own farming business which we both love. And I will probably take on, in the jargon, a couple of interesting for-profits and a couple of interesting not-for-profits. I'm a bit humbled by it, but I've been asked to do an amazing range of things and I'm in the process of finalising very carefully the things I will do where (a) I can make a difference, and (b) which I will find interesting. I'm thankful for those opportunities.

If I were to summarise it from a Christian point of view, there is no such thing as a theology of retirement; not one that I've ever been able to see. I think we need to be active in the pursuit of God's work to the best of our ability for as long as we can. So hopefully I can find other areas to make a contribution.

This is a wonderful country and I rejoice in our prosperity; I think it's a marvellous thing, notwithstanding that there are some people who are still missing out. But can I say that prosperity is not the heart and soul of the nation. Our values, which stem from our beliefs, are what really matter. And we need to pay some serious attention to our beliefs.

Clive Hamilton

Our homes are getting bigger, yet our families are getting smaller. We have more money than previous generations, yet we're more in debt. Our kids go to the best schools money can buy, yet we never see them. What is going wrong? Could it be a nasty case of *affluenza*: an addiction to over-consumption?

Clive Hamilton is an author, academic and intellectual. He founded The Australia Institute think tank, which he directed for fourteen years. Amongst his growing list of published work is the best-selling book, co-authored with Richard Denniss, *Affluenza: When Too Much Is Never Enough.*

Describe the affluenza disease to me.
I think it's an unhealthy preoccupation with money and material things to the point where we invest our hopes and dreams in our consumption activity. Of course, if we do that, they always fail us because we know that's not what life is really about.

Why are we so afflicted by affluenza?
I think it's partly because we've lost track of the things that can really make life worthwhile. People's sense of trying to create an identity has shifted away from community and higher things, and

has been focused more and more on consumption behaviour, status acquired through money, and so on.

There has been, over the last fifteen years in particular, a massive marketing effort designed to persuade us that we can find happiness, identity and meaning in a stainless-steel kitchen or new car. So I think we're witnessing a period of capitalism in which more and more we derive our identity not from what we do, but from what we buy. And the marketers are brilliant at exploiting that.

You talk about the democratisation of luxury as a part of this. Explore that for us.

Well, previously, luxury goods were reserved for the very wealthy, and the great bulk of the population looked on with a sense of awe, envy or derision. But now luxury consumption is available to pretty much everyone because of high and rising incomes in rich countries like Australia. So the luxury goods manufacturers have in a sense come downmarket a bit. They make what they call 'entry level' products. Now you can buy a Louis Vuitton handbag at a price that a shop assistant can aspire to, or a pair of expensive designer sunglasses for $400. I mean, someone with an annual income of $25,000 or $30,000 can aspire to acquire. The manufacturers have made it possible for pretty much anyone to have some taste of luxury. That means that people's aspirations for their consumption have been ratcheted up.

That 'aspiration' word is pretty key in all this. In Affluenza *you raise a question mark over the term 'Aussie Battler'. In reality, do we actually have many Aussie Battlers?*

We don't. Of course we have some, but the concept of Aussies as battlers—as stoic survivors against the hardships of life—is an image we cherish of ourselves as a nation and as a people. But let's face it: the real life of most Australians is one of abundance and luxury. Compare it to how our grandparents lived, even in the 1950s.

Yet, in just the last two days, we have seen this extraordinary outpouring of complaints about how much suffering people are going to have to endure as a result of a 0.25% interest rate rise. The Australian newspaper carried on its front page a huge picture of a couple looking very glum with the corners of their mouths turned down and hugging each other in adversity, standing in front of their house over which they have a one million dollar mortgage. The whole tenor of the article was that these poor people are going to have to cut back on eating out. These people own millions of dollars worth of assets and we are supposed to feel sorry for them because they may have overcommitted themselves, because they are greedy. And yet somehow this passes for part of the national debate that these poor people are suddenly in a difficult situation. Give me a break.

It's interesting to see how our tastes have changed over time. Are we conscious of just how much advertising and branding actually shapes our tastes and desires today?
Well, some of the studies we've done draw out a remarkable fact. If you ask people whether their purchasing behaviour is influenced by advertising nearly all people say, 'No—I don't fall for that sort of stuff. I am an independent person. I make my own choices. I buy what I want.' Then you ask, 'Well, do you think other people are influenced by advertising?' The answer comes back, 'Yes, of course they are. People are so gullible. But not me.' Then you have to ask yourself why—if each person thinks they can't be influenced by advertising—advertisers spend billions of dollars a year trying to change their behaviour. The reason is because it works.

It's interesting that when the advertisers themselves are confronted with the more awful and manipulative aspects of their activities, they deny that their ads actually work. They say, 'Oh no, people aren't influenced by ads.' But I don't think that's what they tell their corporate clients when they're pitching for their business.

In the book you say that even the drug companies have gotten in on the act, creating diseases that their drugs can then treat.
Absolutely. This is a well-established method of big pharma. The major pharmaceutical companies around the world, which really must be the most rapacious companies in the world—it is certainly the most profitable industry in the world—not content to develop cures for existing illnesses, actually manufacture illnesses which they then put out there in the public domain. They create front groups of sufferers of these illnesses who then set up web sites to exchange information, and they work on journalists to start writing stories about how many people are suffering from these illnesses.

One classic case is Female Sexual Dysfunction. Pfizer made a motser from Viagra, and other drug companies looked on in enormous [envy]. They thought, OK, we have to have a women's version of this. So they created this disease, or syndrome, called Female Sexual Dysfunction, and came up with a drug that would solve it. And a lot of people fell for it, including a lot of doctors who are very gullible when duchessed by drug companies.

There are other diseases that they came up with too; normal conditions or unpleasant conditions that suddenly became illnesses that people had to treat with drugs. Like SAD: Social Anxiety Disorder, which we used to call shyness. Even Irritable Bowel Syndrome was medicalised in a way that allowed them to start selling a drug that would cure the problem.

How do you think we can divest ourselves of this disease called affluenza? Part of it is getting correct information, not believing every bit of advertising we hear, having a free press, etc. But what else can we do?
I think we have to recognise that this isn't just advertising. Marketing, which is much broader than advertising, is in our whole culture and is impossible to escape. It's everywhere and it conditions everything. You can't go live in a cave and shut yourself off from the world. You have to cultivate the capacity to constantly have a critical approach and awareness to the messages and the attempts by people to manipulate each of us into behaving in a particular way.

What we must do is become conscious consumers and be constantly monitoring ourselves, asking why we are going to buy something. Is it a need that we actually have or one that has been created? Is it an advertising agency or aspect of popular culture that is exploiting our own inadequacies, neuroses and anxieties? Then we must recognise that we will never be able to solve that inadequacy or anxiety by buying stuff.

So it really means adopting a different sense of self and a different approach to the world. It's hard, but plenty of people do it. And we have a very strong obligation to teach our children how to be critical consumers of media, how to be conscious consumers and always to be suspicious of anyone trying to flog us stuff.

I heard you speak at the 2006 Sydney Writer's Festival. The interesting thing is that my wife and I weren't able to get into the main auditorium because it was full. There were probably a hundred of us sitting outside listening to you via speakers. I wonder if people are starting to wake up to this whole issue.
I think a lot of people are. I think we're seeing an intensification of consumerism, and that will continue, but we are also seeing a reaction

against it. More and more people, quite a slab of the population, are saying, 'No, I don't want to devote my life to superficial and trivial consumption behaviour and the creation of popular culture which is meaningless. I want my life to mean something more than that. I want some depth, I want some understanding, I want some true relationships with other people rather than manufactured ones.' And so I think that is why the *Affluenza* book has done well, because it exposes the tendencies within all of us to seek the superficial as a way out of our daily anxieties. It's very reassuring that more and more people are saying there has to be more to life than the latest consumer gadget, wide screen TV or $700 barbeque.

Joni Eareckson Tada

In 1967 a diving accident left Joni Earekson Tada a quadriplegic. During two years of painful rehabilitation she began the long process of adapting to her wheelchair-bound life, even learning how to paint with a brush held between her teeth. Joni's books have become an inspiration to many, and the feature length film *Joni* has been translated into fifteen languages and brought her worldwide acclaim.

Today the *Joni and Friends* organisation helps thousands of people with disabilities every year. Joni has also become a prominent disability campaigner, well versed in the many bio-ethical dilemmas technology now presents to us, including the use of embryonic stem cells for research.

For those unaware of your background, help us understand just what that day in 1967 was like, and just how difficult that recovery process has been for you.
Well, it was a hot summer day. I went swimming with my sister Cathy and took a dive off this raft that was anchored far off shore of the Chesapeake Bay, and didn't really check the depth of the water. I took the dive and the depth of the water was only about four or five feet. My head hit the bottom, that snapped my neck back and it crushed my fourth and fifth cervical vertebrae, which

severed my spinal cord. And that left me completely paralysed.

I was lying face down in the water, holding my breath, desperately hoping that my sister Cathy would notice that I had not yet surfaced from my dive. Just as I was about to run out of breath, a crab bit my sister's toe. She had her back turned to me, and when that crab bit she whirled around in the water to scream to me to watch out for crabs. She saw that I wasn't on the raft, saw my blond hair floating in the water and came racing after me and pulled me up out of the water. They sent me off to a hospital where I stayed for almost two years.

But that was in 1967, and now almost forty years later—four decades of quadriplegia and living in a wheel chair—I can tell you honestly that I would really rather be in this chair knowing God the way I do, the peace and the comfort that he gives, than to be on my feet without him. I can say that with a smile. That is quite a miracle.

That is indeed a miracle. You came to faith through the accident too.
There were good Christian friends who would come into the hospital and bring pizza and they would bring their guitars and we'd watch soccer matches on Saturday afternoon television. And when they opened up their Bibles they would read to me. At first I wasn't very excited about it because I was quite angry at God. I thought he was the one to blame for this terrible accident. But as they read from the Bible I sensed words of hope, of comfort and consolation, and victory and power to overcome my circumstances—if I would but put my trust and confidence in Jesus Christ who, incidentally, suffered a lot worse than me. So as I did that, I began to sense a freedom inside my heart, an uncanny ability to embrace the circumstances I found myself in. That Bible catapulted me into a journey with Jesus which grows each and every day.

Before your accident, what did you hope to be? What dreams did you have?
Believe it or not, I wanted to be a physiotherapist. Isn't that something?

It's ironic.
I ended up getting into physiotherapy except on the wrong end, so to speak.

What have you learnt then through all of this about God's destiny for people? You wouldn't want to say that this was God's perfect will for you, but he has certainly used you in such an amazing way as a result.
Well, sometimes God's will involves some pretty painful things. When you think of it, it was God's will that Jesus go to the cross. It was part of the perfect plan of salvation, yet going to that cross involved murder, torture and injustice; it involved treason on behalf of Judas Iscariot. We look at that those things and we think, how can any of that be God's will? Yet God permits what he hates to accomplish marvellous things that he loves. God did not take delight in my spinal cord injury, but nevertheless he allowed it. It was his will, and the long-range plan and purpose was that I might be drawn closer to my Saviour. So even in my own life God has permitted what he hated, this quadriplegia, to produce something that he loves, and that is the image of his son in my life.

You would've wrestled with the whole 'why hasn't God healed me' question too. I believe you even visited Kathryn Kuhlman, the well-known healer back in the early days.
Oh my goodness, I went to so many faith healers. I got anointed by oil, I confessed my sins, I did everything and anything. I followed

every single scriptural injunction. I believed with a capital B. I had faith to the extent that I was calling my friends on the telephone and explaining to them that the next time they saw me they'd see me on my feet. I really was way out there on the limb with my confidence that Christ would heal me, but he didn't. My feet and my fingers never got the message that my heart and head kept saying.

Christians sometimes want to erase suffering out of the dictionary. If you read the Bible you will see that it is often God's best tool to make us more like Jesus. The choice is simply ours to yield to it and to allow him to use that suffering rather than complaining, avoiding it, escaping it, divorcing it—we've got all kinds of solutions for suffering except to embrace it as God's will for our life. But when we do, what a difference his grace makes.

You and Christopher Reeve had your disability in common when Reeve was still with us. But he was an ardent supporter of embryonic stem cell research and cloning, while you're an opponent of it, even though some would say that could be your cure. Why are you so concerned about embryonic stem cell research?

As a person with a disability believe me I watch very, very closely the advancements in any medical therapy for someone in my condition. And I'm here to tell you that the best kind of stem cell research is research using stem cells from your own adult tissue. Adult stem cell therapies are being developed right now—569 adult stem cell-related clinical trials going on in the United States, for coronary heart disease, multiple sclerosis, vascular disease, brain injury, Type 1 diabetes, stroke, spinal cord injury, Huntington's disease. Embryonic stem cell research hasn't even come through with a successful proof of concept experiment in a rat. So, number one, I am very excited about stem cell research and I want to support stem cell research that is not only most promising but is most cost effective, most safe and most ethical.

Which brings me to my second point. I have been paralysed for almost forty years, Sheridan, and I would love to walk again, honestly I would. But not at any price. I think it is more important to bequeath to this world a moral compass. When people start killing human life in order to gain a cure, that kind of exploitation is very, very dangerous to people like me with disabilities because the weak and the vulnerable are always exposed in a society that thinks nothing of destroying human life. If we violate human embryos today we become callous, we become inured to transgressing the unborn child with a disability, then the infant with a disability, then the elderly. Already around the world they are labelling people who are in comas as 'post-persons' and infants born with severe disabilities as 'pre-persons'. As a quadriplegic I don't want to live in a world where the pharmaceutical and bio-tech industries set the moral agenda.

The nation of Germany—which, incidentally, is most curious because they have suffered through their error of wrong thinking with social eugenics and genetic engineering in the 1940s—is the nation setting the standard [in bioethics] now. They prohibit cloning; they strictly limit in-vitro fertilisation production to only two to three embryos and all of them must be implanted, not discarded. I think they have learned their lesson as a nation and I just wish that we would gain and glean from their example.

It could be argued that therapeutic cloning is potentially giving life to people with chronic illnesses and disabilities like yours, and therefore is good. What's your response to that?
I don't want human life to be killed in order to benefit me in this

wheelchair. And so-called cures which might come out of stem cell research using human embryos is far, far down the road—perhaps twenty or thirty years from now—whereas right now we are experiencing some incredible medical treatments. I have a friend who had an adult stem cell therapy treatment done on her broken neck. She travelled to Portugal for the operation. Stem cells were scraped from her own nasal tissue and they were pressed into the injured area of her spinal cord, and now nine months later Lara can feel in her legs and she can take a few halting steps using crutches. That is nothing short of a miracle. Why it is that the media doesn't talk about these amazing advancements is beyond me.

The other issue connected to this discussion is euthanasia. In some countries assisted suicide has been legalised; for other countries it remains a matter of debate. What do you say to somebody who is in such chronic pain they just want to die?
For one thing, when someone with a disability or a terminal disease is in that much pain and agony, I think the fundamental issue is not that they want to die but they want relief from pain. They don't want to be socially isolated. They want to know that they are not alone in their affliction. When I was first injured—a quadriplegic lying in bed for a full year, hooked up to tubes and machines, paralysed and unable to even lift my head off the pillow for an entire year—believe me, I wanted to end my life too. But my problem back then was not my quadriplegia. It was my depression. There are cures for depression, so I think that we need to remember that the quick fix is not three grams of Phenobarbital in the veins. That's not compassion.

Compassion is sitting by the bedside of a despairing person who is in pain and ascribing positive meaning to their situation.

Treatment is educating doctors on how to prescribe good pain management. It's donating to the hospice movement in your city or your community. Physician-assisted suicide is the epitome of abandonment to a person with a disability. I'm disabled, I'm in a wheelchair, I'm a quadriplegic—I've been there. But one is not better off dead than disabled. Better that we ascribed positive meaning to the pain. Keep that person from becoming socially isolated. Give them the psychological and social support they need and get them connected to caring Christians who will pray for them and come alongside and show them the prince of life, the resurrection of life—Jesus who has the words of life and is the way, the truth and the life. Our adversary the devil is a murderer, but Jesus can give grace, power and strength that will see anybody through the worst times of affliction.

Let's make that Christian compassion, and not a bottle full of pills or a lethal injection.

John Eldredge

St Irenaeus famously said, 'The glory of God is man fully alive.' For John Eldredge that phrase has become something of a mission statement—seeing men and women come 'fully alive as the image-bearers of a breathtaking God', as he puts it. As founder and director of Ransomed Heart Ministries in Colorado Springs, Colorado, John is the author of numerous books, including *Epic, Waking the Dead*, the best-selling *Wild At Heart* and most recently *Walking With God*.

When John joined us on Open House, our conversation focused on his desire to see true masculinity rediscovered in both church and world.

Haven't those books of yours done well? I'm thinking particularly of Wild at Heart *and* Waking the Dead. *They've gone through the roof all around the world.*
Much to my surprise. They really seem to have touched a chord. I feel like the fellow in the parable that found treasure in the field. I knew it was treasure, I just didn't know if anybody else would think it was treasure.

Wild at Heart is about the 'secret' to a man's soul. I wonder if it's resonated so well because to some degree we have feminised the Christian faith over the years.

Oh, Sheridan, in a big way. You know, our image of Jesus, the way we hold up a certain kind of man in the church as a model of masculinity—it's all been reduced to something kind of lifeless and very, very *nice*. I think there are a lot of guys out there saying, 'I can't relate to that; that doesn't speak to me; that doesn't answer my questions. Who is going to show me what it means to be a man?' Those were *my* questions.

My producer and I were talking about the way the church can come across to the male mind. The décor of the average church interior is pastel colours. There are often flowers on the front pulpit area.
Oh yeah.

We sing songs like 'Jesus Lover of my Soul' and other love songs to Jesus. I don't know about you but as a man I often cringe at those songs. Compare those with some of the popular hymns of the past, like 'Onward Christian Soldiers'—songs very much about action.
Right! 'Marching as to war . . .'

Is that part of the problem?
It is, Sheridan. The church right now almost has a feminine soul to it and church leaders will tell you, 'We can't get men to volunteer for leadership', 'we can't get them to come to our programs'. So it tends to be the women that run the programs and end up shaping the ethos of the church.

In Wild at Heart *you say that men basically need three things: a battle to fight, a beauty to rescue and an adventure to live. How did you come to those three?*
In a couple of different ways. First, go and watch little boys for a

while. Just spend an hour watching them play. They want battles and adventures and then they want to rescue the damsel in distress.

Then, look at the movies that men like: *Gladiator, Braveheart, Chariots of Fire, The Shawshank Redemption*. In any of these stories those are always the key ingredients.

Then it was just my own heart. I found myself saying, 'God put these deep desires in my heart and what does Christianity have to do with any of that?' Where are the great battles for us to fight? Where is the adventure? I just don't want to learn five principles of marriage communication. What does it mean to rescue this woman that God has given me?

A friend and I were talking about this issue of men in the church and he began telling me about his brother, a very manual guy, who hasn't gone on in his Christian faith. 'On the weekends he tinkers around with cars,' my friend told me. 'I wonder if the church had some sort of service ministry, perhaps to single parents who can't afford to look after their cars, or maybe a home renovation ministry, maybe then he'd get fired up.' I wonder if the male soul in particular wants to be active, not simply to sit, stagnate and receive information, but to get in there and do something.

Sheridan, bingo! I mean, just get guys together and they don't typically sit around in a circle sharing their feelings. The typical kind of small group, Sunday school, Bible class model just doesn't work with men. They want to be out; they want to be doing something. It's fascinating though. If you can get guys together fixing a car or stacking a pile of wood, shooting a basketball, anything, they *will* start talking to each other. But it has to be around some kind of external activity.

Men are made to move, right? And Adam's basic sin, if you

go back to that story in Genesis, is the sin of passivity. Eve is being tempted, Satan is there about to take down the human race, and Adam doesn't move. He doesn't speak, he doesn't act, and that passivity that crept into the life of men is the problem. We have got to tap into that part of them that knows that they're made to move.

Of course, there is a question mark over all of this. While Wild at Heart *has been so successful, there has been some polarisation over it. Some men have found it liberating; others have found it a bit stereotypical. They've felt, well, I'm not the mountain-climbing, adrenalin-seeking, chest-thumping kind of bloke that's described in* Wild At Heart. *How do you respond to the idea that* Wild at Heart *could just be a stereotype of masculinity?*

People need to know some things. I weigh 135 pounds. I've never played football. I don't drive a truck with big tyres on it. I don't have the heads of dead animals on the wall in my house. I'm not the guy that would come across as your sort of macho guy, you know. I never was a Navy Seal. I've never been in the armed forces. But here's the deal: the masculine soul *is* universal because we are made in the image of God, and in the first chapter of Genesis it says either male or female [are made in his image]. God says right there, gender is really important.

So, right, some men don't want a literal battle to fight. They don't like the movie *Braveheart* and they don't want to go to war. But some of those same men are doctors and they fight every day for the health of their patients. There is something in them that is very fierce when someone's life is on the line. Or some of them are teachers and they are battling for the hearts of their students so that these kids hang in there and get an education. They give their life to that. That universal desire is there. Let me take adventure. Some guys don't want to jump off cliffs or kayak or whatever. But some of my friends are really into finance and they love investing and they are on the internet doing all that. That is high risk adventure. It just expresses itself in different ways.

A battle to fight, an adventure to live—and a beauty to rescue. How does that last one work for the man called to singleness?
Yeah, that's a really good question. The reason we have that duty to rescue is immense because God does. Jesus fights for his bride, the church, right? And the church is a lot of people. So I think there is something in the heart of men that wants to help others. Just take any situation where men are called to come through for those who are maybe less fortunate financially or in a hard situation emotionally. It takes a man to come through and help someone else. That's love. That's love in action. He may not be fighting for a specific woman but he is fighting for God's beauty—fighting for the church.

John, you call your organisation Ransomed Heart Ministries. Tell me the significance of that phrase.
Thanks for asking that. We have really lost this, Sheridan. First, we have lost the idea that the heart is central. If you go back and look at the Scriptures, the heart is absolutely central to what God is after. Jesus says that his people honoured him with their lips but their hearts were far from him. 'You shall love the Lord your God with all *heart*, soul, mind and strength.' Proverbs 4:23 says, 'Watch over your heart above all else for out of your heart flows the wellspring of life'. What happens to a person's heart is what happens to that person.

Part two of this is that we have also lost the idea that Jesus came to redeem, or ransom, our hearts. Ezekiel 36:26 says, 'A new heart I will give you', and Jeremiah 31 says, 'I'm going to make a new covenant with my people and I'll write my law on their hearts'. And then Paul says in Ephesians 3, 'God comes to dwell in our hearts', and Jesus says in Luke 8 that the seed that fell on good soil stands for those with a 'noble and good heart' who hear the word, receive it and by perseverance produce a crop. So all we are trying to say is that the beauty of the gospel is that God comes to ransom our hearts. He comes to rescue us at the deepest possible level of our being, down deep inside.

This would say something about understanding our passions and desires—something you talk a lot about in your books. I think many of us have felt that anything we really desire or want could be coming from our sinful nature. You can go too far as well and say that everything we feel or want is from God. How do you discern what is of ego and what is of the redeemed heart that God has created within us?
I think we have to start with what the Psalm says: 'Delight yourself in the Lord and he will give you the desires of your heart.' It has to start with loving God, and if we don't love God—I mean, really genuinely love him—sorting out the rest is going to be pretty hard because all kinds of things in our lives try and present themselves as God to us. People make gods out of all kinds of things—their work, another person, their marriage. Some people make their children their god. So we have got to have God first.

But as we have God first we discover that he does write these deep passions on our hearts. Paul says in his writings, look, the desires of the flesh are really evident: anger, greed, lust, idolatry. Those are not hard things to figure out. You get a guy who says,

'Hey, it's on my heart to run away with my secretary.' That's a no-brainer; it's not from God. But there are these desires in our hearts that *are* from God. What is so beautiful about this is if we can recover the deep and holy desires of our hearts we'd actually find God's calling for our life.

For years I felt very guilty that I did not want to be a missionary. When I became a Christian at nineteen and I looked around the church, the message was pretty clear: if you are really committed, if you really want to serve God, you'll be a missionary. And I felt terrible that I didn't want to be. And I thought, that's what I should go do because I don't want to do it and therefore it would be more noble.

Yeah, that's right.
Could you imagine how awful that would be to be the mission of that person who doesn't want to minister to you? There are miserable missionaries out there: I'm just doing it because I'm supposed to; I have no joy in it whatsoever. But I realised that that wasn't my calling. What I love to do is to counsel and to write and to speak to people about the heart of God. That gets me out of bed in the morning. I can't wait to do that. And what's funny is you put me in any situation and that's what I will start doing, because that's my calling. So if we can help people understand that they have these desires: for some it's to start an inner city basketball clinic for kids, for others it's becoming a musician, for someone else it's a compelling desire to be a teacher. That's your calling from God.

A friend wrote me an email recently. He said, 'I really want to know what those passions in my heart are. I'm not really in touch with them.' How do you even begin to discern what your God-given passions are?

That's getting the cart ahead of the horse, as the saying goes. Jesus said that he came to heal the broken-hearted and to set the captive free. Again, in so many of those Old Testament promises he says he wants to give us a new heart. You really have to begin with the work of Christ in restoring our hearts. Recovering passion and desire is a part of that. But if you try and start with the fruit of it, that is going to be difficult to do.

I think it is important to ask ourselves what makes us come alive. What do you dream about? What do you tend to get angry about? What injustices? Those sorts of things. But I think it is far more fruitful to go to God and say, 'Lord, I want that Isaiah 61 ministry in my heart. I pray that you would come, Jesus, and begin your healing work in my heart.' As we pray that and invite that ministry of Christ, suddenly we start uncovering all the desires that have long gone dead, and new desires that he gives to us. But it really comes out of the ministry of Christ in us versus something that you sort of have to go figure out.

What advice do you have for those wanting to engage men with the local church?
I'll offer some very frank advice. First, get rid of all the religious language. Men don't talk like that, people don't talk like that. You know, 'We are going to press into the holy of holies, brothers.' Guys kind of look at each other and go, *What is he talking about?* So if you want to connect with guys you've got to strip it of the religious language.

Secondly, in the light of that, offer genuine masculine fellowship. Real camaraderie. Guys don't get together and just sing hymns. That's just not what they do naturally. Genuine worship of God will come, but you can't start there. Again, it's putting the cart before the horse. Get guys together and talk about things that are real.

Thirdly, your leadership has to be masculine. [Leaders] have got to be real men who are honest men, not guys who are faking it. Honestly, most guys are posers. We are. We are scared to death that we are not what we ought to be as men and so we fake it. We fake that we have a better marriage than we do, we fake that we have a deeper spirituality than we do. The leadership can't be faking. They have got to be honest guys who are the real deal because men know. You can tell who's the real deal and who's not.

If you do those three things you will create contacts for men to come together. I loved your idea that maybe there is a ministry of fixing cars for single moms, building houses with Habit for Humanity, or something. Give guys something to do. They have got to have a project.

Tim Flannery

GHOST CITIES AND LOST SPECIES

Nine of the ten warmest years on record have occurred in the past fifteen years. In the 1960s seven million people were affected by flood each year; today that number is 150 million. Since 1994 the number of category four and five hurricanes has almost doubled. Looking ahead, some suggest there will be no ice in the Arctic and no polar bears left by the year 2050.

Tim Flannery is a leading thinker in environmental science. His book *The Weather Makers* has disturbed many, showing just what the future may hold should the much talked about environmental crisis reach its worst-case scenario. I spoke to him in September 2006, just as environmental concern was finally making regular media headlines.

The people I know who have read The Weather Makers *have been quite shaken as a result. Do you ever feel like a prophet of doom?*
I'm not sure about a prophet of doom, but I know what they're feeling. As I was researching the book I went through a period when I actually felt quite depressed. I'm not normally a depressive person, but for twelve months or so I was really struggling getting out of bed in the morning and thinking, 'It can't possibly be this bad.' It was only when I came to think about solutions that I started feeling energised again.

You've suggested that in fifty year's time Perth could be the first 'ghost city'. Is that still your view?
Well, I think there is going to be a bit of competition in the race. I didn't foresee Hurricane Katrina's impact on New Orleans at that point. But if you imagine a second hurricane hitting that city, then it may well beat Perth to the finish line. I was there recently and it's incredible. There are 70,000 houses totally destroyed, another 70 or 80,000 severely damaged, and the maximum number of houses ever built in New Orleans in a year was 2800. So there are many, many years of reconstruction to go and that area is just becoming a shooting gallery for hurricanes.

Perth's water supply is desperate. This year has seen the lowest rainfall since records were kept, going back to 1836.

What do you think Australia could look like then in fifty years' time if we don't do anything?
Let's start with the shape of the continent, because the shape of the continent may change significantly as sea levels rise.

It is very hard to put a timeline on the rising oceans because no one can really say how stable or unstable some of the major ice sheets are, like the Greenland ice sheet. But let's assume they melt. We will have significant incursions. In fifty years we could be looking at sea levels several metres higher than they are today. So a lot of low-lying Australia will vanish under the waves. You can imagine the impact that will have on coastal infrastructure, whether it is ports or coastal cities or just houses by the sea.

Of course, there will be many other parts of the world equally affected. In Bangladesh there are 120 million people in that tiny country; 10 million of them live within one metre of sea level. Where are they going to go as the ocean rises? We'll expect to see a lot more international migration and a breakdown in international law and order. It's not going to be a very pleasant world that we leave to our children unless we can get on top of this problem.

Where will the deserts be?
It's a very good question; we're trying to understand that at the moment. It is interesting that across north-western Australia rainfall is increasing as tropical cyclones become more prevalent. But across eastern and southern Australia rainfall is dropping precipitously, with the biggest losses in some parts of the east coast—the Brisbane area and Sydney area for example. They look set to become much, much drier. So my prediction is that the deserts will move eastwards.

Let's talk about the number of species that we've lost. Have you got those figures on hand?
Yeah, well at the moment we are beginning to see the impacts on species extinction. So we have lost several species of frogs now, including Australia's Gastric Brooding Frog, which was an incredible creature. It used to brood its young in its stomach which had turned into a sort of brood pouch during the breeding season. It's now gone.

If we look elsewhere around the world we see really significant impacts. The polar bears are under such enormous stress at the moment. This year we have seen the first hybrid polar bear ever recorded—between a brown bear and a polar bear—because the polar bears are spending more time on land around garbage dumps and whatever else. We've seen the first cases of polar bear cannibalism, where male bears have been jumping on the breeding dens of females, caving them in and eating the females and the cubs. And we've seen the first cases of polar bears drowning in the

Arctic Ocean—the first that have been recorded by Inuit people.

If things continue as they are, the best estimates are that we stand to lose probably seven out of every ten species on the planet.

What about in fifty years?
It's hard to confirm timelines. When I wrote the book, the best science was suggesting that the Arctic ice cap might have melted away entirely by about 2100 or 2050. Just ten months after I finished the book a new study came out and said that current rates of melt are so high that we expect now that there will be no ice in the Artic by 2030. As we speak on the phone now, there is another study in press by the US Navy suggesting that because of the ingress of warm water from the North Pacific there may be no polar ice cap in summer as early as 2016. Things could be catastrophically bad by 2050. If we are lucky and we have done the right thing in terms of reducing emissions we may be facing smaller changes.

Tim, is there any chance you could be wrong?
Yes, there is. No one can predict the future. I sincerely hope that I am proved wrong on some of this stuff. The trajectories, year after year, are pointing all in the same direction—that we have underestimated climate change and its impact on the planet. The basic science is very simple: the atmosphere is a very small place overall; it's only one five-hundredth as big as the oceans and therefore it's easy to pollute. And these greenhouse gases, they are so voluminous. You burn a tonne of coal and you end up, paradoxically, with two or three tonnes of carbon dioxide going into the atmosphere, because those little coal atoms attach to larger oxygen atoms to form a very big waste stream and that carbon dioxide just keeps the heat close to the surface of the planet.

Is it all down to CO₂ levels? Is that the ultimate culprit?

Carbon dioxide is responsible for 80% of the warming we see. It's very interesting the way it works; the carbon dioxide itself only warms the atmosphere a little bit, but that little bit of warming allows more water vapour to be held in the atmosphere and water vapour is a very powerful greenhouse gas. So it amplifies the initial change caused by the CO_2. Some of the other culprits are methane, which is twenty times more powerful than carbon dioxide as a greenhouse gas but much rarer, thankfully; and it's responsible for about 18% of the rest of the warming. And then the 2% remaining, there are a few other really bizarre chemicals like chlorofluorocarbons (CFCs)—the problem that caused the ozone hole. Some of them are 10,000 times more powerful than carbon dioxide as a greenhouse gas, but they are very rare, thankfully.

We heard news reports recently that the hole in the ozone layer has stabilised and may actually close by the year 2060. What do you think of that?

It is some of the best news we have had in climate science for a very, very long time. The chemical that was destroying the ozone layer—the CFCs—were banned by an international treaty called the Montreal Protocol, in 1987. It's taken us nearly twenty years to see the benefit of that very insightful action. If that hadn't happened, the world we would be living in today would be a very different place, I can tell you. You wouldn't be using the beach in Melbourne. In fact, it goes further than that, because that little layer of ozone just a few millimetres thick in total protects us from most of the ultra violet radiation that comes from the sun. With that sort of ultra violet radiation our bodies are subject to cancers, blindness rates go up, crops fail to grow, the oceans become very severely impacted. So we were just so lucky that that international treaty was signed into law.

In The Weather Makers *you also raise the question as to whether humans have already tipped the switch to create an ice-free earth. Have we tripped the switch to the point where we can't trip it back again?*
I really, really hope not. But the answer is I don't know, and nobody else really knows. The world's foremost climate expert in this area is a man called Dr James Hanson who heads the Goddard Institute at NASA. He is now saying that we either already have or are perilously close to triggering a 25-metre rise in sea levels. If you look at a big building near the ocean, and look eight stories up that building, that's about where the sea level will be.

Let's talk about some of the possible things we can do to reduce the problem. What about the various forms of alternative energy? In the end, can we ultimately cut out coal as a source of energy?
Well, I think conventional burning of coal has to be cut out. Whether we can sequester the carbon dioxide from burning coal under the ground or not is an open question at the moment. But it is very hard to say which of those many, many alternatives are actually going to be the most cost-effective way in any situation to generate electricity. But there is only one way to find out and that is to get the polluter to pay and let the well-regulated free market work out where the new wealth is going to be made.

What do you think about nuclear?
Well, the same argument. We have got to have a well-regulated marketplace; make sure the cost of carbon is included. Make sure that we've got a well-regulated trade that doesn't let uranium fall

into the hands of the people we don't want to have it. Add up all those costs and see if it actually stacks up.

Of course, one of the questions about nuclear is whether it could have other negative ramifications for us.
Exactly. I mean, nuclear power is a more difficult option, partly because of the waste, and partly because of its links with bombs and nuclear proliferation. They are not insurmountable difficulties but they are considerable difficulties, I think anyone would admit. I think we need to simply cost out very carefully what it actually costs to run a well-regulated nuclear industry and then we go in eyes wide open if we decide to embark on that industry. We know where we stand.

There are also questions whether something like wind-generated power can actually produce enough energy to be worth it in the end. What are your thoughts there?
There is so much misinformation out there. Really. I mean, you hear about birds running into wind farms. That problem was effectively solved twenty years ago. There is still the odd incident, but nothing like in the past. Even hybrid fuel cars, you find the opponents of those telling the most outrageous lies about how inefficient they are and whatever.

So the only way to find out about this is, as I say, tax the polluter, get the polluter to pay and then let the free market sort out where the new wealth is going to be created. When I go to Europe and look at the billions that are being invested in the new energy economy, you realise how backwards this country is.

What can everyday individuals do to try and create a more positive future than what you've outlined in the book and for us this evening?

Every time we have a cup of tea with the electric kettle, or have a shower if you have an electric hot water system, the pollution you create is still going to be in the atmosphere in a century's time, damaging your grandchildren's future. So there is a strong imperative for us all to act and do something about this.

The things you can do are so easy. If you own your own house and you need to replace your hot water system, get a solar hot water system. Almost anywhere in Australia it will deliver free hot water for you for most of the year. About half your power bill is just keeping that old electric kettle going in the roof. It's mad.

If you're thinking about buying a new car buy the most energy-efficient motor vehicle you can lay your hands on. The same is true for any electrical goods that you buy; go out of your way to find out what the most efficient goods are. It's cheaper in the long term. If you are renting or find it difficult to buy, make those infrastructure changes. Ring up your energy provider and ask for a green energy option. For the cost of a cup of coffee a day in some instances, or a week in others, you can have a totally clean source for your electricity.

But also when you go to the supermarket. If you buy a mango that has been imported from the Philippines or Mexico, well, that has been carried, using fossil fuel, half way around the world. If you buy something produced locally, going to a farmer's market or growing something in your garden, there is no cost for fossil fuel.

So it's everything from your shopping patterns and food through to your electricity and transport. All are important to consider in this.

I know it's hard to predict the future, but if we do nothing how many years do you give the human race?
Look, I think humanity will survive. But what will be destroyed

is this amazing performance that we call civilisation. Civilisation as we know it depends on enormous resources—fresh water in the right places at the right time, food, stable sea levels so we can have an international shipping trade. You can't pick up cities and move them if the ocean starts to rise or the resources go away. So civilisation will be the victim, and my nightmare scenario is that, by Australia selling its coal and uranium overseas, we will trigger a climate instability that brings on a dark age, and that dark age will be peopled with individuals who still have the means for making the most powerful and destructive weapons that humanity has ever devised.

Well, let's work to make sure that doesn't come to pass.
It's just so simple. Really, the challenge isn't that great. We've just got to get the awareness.

Jeffrey Sachs

ENDING EXTREME POVERTY IS THE GREAT OPPORTUNITY OF
OUR TIME

Professor Jeffrey Sachs is to nations what doctors are to people. His extensive career has seen him advise more than one hundred countries on how to reduce poverty. He's advised former UN Secretary General Kofi Annan and has even given economic lessons to U2's Bono.

Professor Sachs is Director of the Earth Institute at Columbia University. From 2002 to 2006 he was Director of the United Nations' Millennium Project, a plan to see global poverty and hunger halved by 2015. His widely-read books include *The End of Poverty* and *Common Wealth*. When Professor Sachs joined us in early 2007, he told us why he believed extreme poverty could be brought to an end as soon as 2025.

It's certainly an ambitious plan—to see extreme poverty eliminated by 2025. What needs to happen for the goal to be reached?
The good news is that a lot of poverty is being ended by the wonders of modern technology and the good side of globalisation. There has been rapid economic growth through Asia, and poverty rates and absolute numbers living in extreme poverty are decreasing significantly in China, India and throughout South East Asia. Unfortunately there are regions of the world where extreme poverty

has so far proved resistant to the forces of globalisation—where market forces are bypassing people and where the suffering is extreme.

The key is to get those parts of the world connected to the positive drive of the world economy and the positive momentum of technology. If Africa, Central Asia, parts of South America—especially the Andes region—can get connected to global trade and investment the same way as the dynamic parts of Asia have, we will see the end of poverty. The point of my book is that it won't happen automatically. We have to help make it happen.

When you have corrupt regimes in place like Robert Mugabe's in Zimbabwe, can any of those things ever happen?
Of course governments are able to destroy the chances [of success], and unfortunately we have enough thugs around. But people need to understand that the issue goes well beyond the problems of governance. There are well-governed places that are impoverished for other reasons. Maybe malaria and AIDS are holding these places back. Maybe it's a lack of basic infrastructure such as roads and electricity, the lack of access to safe drinking water, or, what is often the case, very fragile agriculture through significant drought.

The cliché that the poor are just the victims of their own government is too simple. The poor can also be victims of climate, disease, lack of infrastructure and so on. Those are solvable problems and we can help them solve those problems.

So your idea is to focus on those kinds of combatable issues and wait for those regimes to change?
Absolutely. You made the analogy to a medical doctor, and I like that analogy. In my book I talk about clinical economics. I have

watched my wife, a wonderful clinician and paediatrician, do her work over the last twenty-five years and it has always impressed me how, in order to treat a child, you have to know the details of the specific ailment. You have to know the conditions of the family. You have to interpret things very carefully. A fever isn't just a fever; it has to be understood at its root cause.

Similarly, with extreme poverty we need to get away from the simplistic idea that extreme poverty is simply the fault of one thing. We need to do a kind of differential diagnosis, understand what the sources of the problem are, and work with those problems that are solvable. In my experience, in most parts of the world, extreme poverty could be brought down significantly by the application of proven straight-forward investments in the right places.

What kind of investments are you talking about?
Let me take the case of the Millennium Villages. We are working in twelve regions in sub-Saharan Africa that are among the very poorest in the world. In all of these cases the people are suffering from a profound lack of basic productivity. They don't grow enough food to even stay alive, much less to earn a surplus that they can bring to the market and so start climbing out of poverty. Though they differ according to the specific geography and ecology, the targets for investment are to raise farming productivity, and to help people have access to basic health care. Health care is a direct input to wellbeing, but it also raises productivity. Investments in schools and school feeding programs are also important so that the children have enough nourishment to learn. There needs to be basic infrastructure: a road, some connection to electricity to manage pumps or refrigeration in a clinic or to recharge a telephone which might be the single life-line of connection for a whole village to

the rest of the nation or the world. So basic interventions are in agriculture, in public health, in education and in infrastructure, meaning roads, power, water, sanitation.

When you look at the cost of those interventions they turn out to be remarkably small compared to the benefits. In the case of the Millennium Villages Project, the investment is fifty dollars per person per year in these villages brought in from the outside, and when combined with resources in the villages and at the national level and from other partner organisations, it is amazing to see how a little can go an enormous way to save lives, help children grow up healthy, and give impoverished communities a chance to move forward.

Do we need more foreign aid from more Western countries?
Our own countries are so rich right now. It would take significantly less than 1% of income to be able to get the bed nets, fertilisers, medicines, pumps, to get the roads paved and the clinics filled. That would spell the difference not only between life and death but between economic development and continued extreme poverty. So it would not take the rich world much.

If this were done on a voluntary basis, wonderful. But the fact of the matter is that it's not being done on a voluntary basis. That means that government has to pick up the responsibility. Our governments, to be honest about it, have recognised this all along. They have promised time and again to give 0.7% of gross national product as official aid. Australia has made the promise; the United States has made the promise; indeed, all the high-income countries have made the promise. But only five of them have lived up to the promise: Sweden, Norway, Denmark, Netherlands and Luxembourg. Several other European countries are now on track to reach 0.7%. The whole European Union has promised that core members will give 0.7% of national income as official aid by 2015. But that is not a great record for other donor countries. We promised but we are not delivering.

I was in Jogjakarta, Indonesia, in 2007 and got talking to folks affected by the earthquake there in May 2006. Their complaint was that while aid had been given, little of it reached them. Money seemed to get siphoned off as it passed through various government agencies. How do we actually get the money to the people who need it?

The key is to have a program approach that works right in the communities themselves. That's what the Millennium Villages do.

We shouldn't just give a transfer of money. We should be helping with specific needs. Again, agriculture, the health sector, education of children, basic infrastructure are the things that the poorest countries need. Beyond that they really have to have their own leadership and responsibility to develop the private sector and to undertake economic growth.

What concerns me, and what I would like people to understand, is that when you have nothing you can't get started on your own. You need a helping hand and that is what foreign aid should be all about. It's not simply redistribution of income. It is helping to empower the poor so that they can escape from the trap of poverty and get on a path of economic development.

The more practical and holistic the approach is—in other words, targeting several key sectors simultaneously in a mutually reinforcing way—the faster and more reliably this is going to happen.

So in terms of foreign aid we can encourage our governments to stay true to their promises, and even increase their promises. What about individuals? What part can we play in the grand plan of eliminating extreme poverty by 2025?

I think individuals should first of all learn about these commitments. Learn about the Millennium Development Goals. Learn about how straight-forward it is in fact to make a major difference. Then support some of those programs, whether it's the Millennium Villages or donations of anti-malaria bed nets or the Global Fund to fight AIDS, TB and malaria. If we all gave, out of our own generosity, 0.7% of our incomes, well, that would do the job.

In your mind, what role do churches play in the fight against poverty?

The churches have two enormous roles to play. They have, out of the tenets of their religion, a major commitment to helping the poor. And there are major church movements that collect resources and donate for the poor. The churches also operate as a service delivery mechanism. If you go to almost any impoverished rural area in Africa there is a church. That church may be helpful in distributing anti-malaria bed nets, or helping with water, or running the local clinic. Many, many denominations are playing an important role in this. And it works at both ends. Churches in most cases are international organisations; they reach us in our own communities and they reach the poorest of the poor in their communities.

You have said that ending poverty is the great opportunity of our time. Why do you think we are the generation that can see the end of extreme poverty?

It's the wealth that we have, the power of technology, and that we have already reduced poverty in so many places in the world means that for the first time in history we have the tools. There is enough literacy and technological connectivity in the poor countries that a modest effort by the rich countries mobilising these proven technologies could end extreme poverty. That is the first time this can be said. Go back thirty or forty years: China was so poor and so numerous, as were so many other parts of the world that are now getting out of extreme poverty, that the burden implied for the rich countries would have been much greater than could have been mustered.

However there is now enough wealth and capable technology, that if we just make a modest effort in the rich world we will have a decisive effect for the benefit of the poor. We have just got to stop turning our backs on this issue and face it straight on. We have to tell our own [national leaders] that the only way this world is going to be safe is not through the military approach, but by investing in peace and investing in development.

Jeffrey, I'm sure you could be earning a lot more money than you're making now, sitting on a handful of company boards somewhere. Why are you doing what you're doing? Why do you feel this role is yours to run with?

Can you imagine anything more compelling in life than the opportunity to be helpful? I can't actually imagine it. It is true that being a financial expert, a monetary expert and so on, there are definitely alternative opportunities. But I find this opportunity to really help problems of extreme poverty simply the most meaningful way to live life that I can imagine. I know this is true of a lot of other people. I have wonderful colleagues from the business community who were making huge amounts of money and decided that what they really wanted to do with their lives was devote them to using their great business skills to help solve problems like this.

We have more than we need in the rich world. We have this opportunity to give something. It is an extremely exhilarating feeling to see that it is possible not only to give but actually help real progress.

Was there a moment of epiphany for you when you changed direction?
I went into economics because I was hoping this profession would give tools which would be useful for the world. So I did go into the field with some hope that it could be not just a theoretical field but something useful.

After a few years of being a Professor at Harvard University, I was invited to give some policy advice to Bolivia which was in very deep crisis. Lo and behold, I saw that the things I had learned could actually help solve a critical problem. I got hooked, and I worked on many, many dozens of countries around the world, looking at problems of inflation, instability, currency crises and trade reform. Then about a dozen years ago I began working in Africa and the nature of the problems there were so severe and the crisis of disease was so great that it opened up a new chapter for me.

The poorest places in Africa are really unlike any other part of the world.

Wess Stafford

Around the globe thousands of children are victimised by a lack of food, education and protection; by war, pornography and prostitution. These children rarely cry out, yet in just a few short years the world's problems will be on their shoulders. Humanity's future rests upon them.

Wess Stafford is the CEO of Compassion International, which today has over one million children sponsored in twenty-six developing countries. He believes it's time for a paradigm shift: children are too important—and too intensely loved by God—to be left behind or left to chance. His touching and tragic childhood experiences in a West African village shaped him to become a champion for the forgotten children of world poverty. As you read on, you may well be moved to do the same.

Your book Too Small to Ignore *is a very moving description of how you grew up on the Ivory Coast of Africa. Just how different would that upbringing have been had you grown up in your place of birth—the United States?*
About as different as you could possibly get. I know I sit here looking an awful lot like an American. I'm not American at all. I'm African.

In your heart?

In every way, actually. I think that God had his hand on me when I was five years old, preparing me for the job that I have today. When I was born all the hosts of heaven must've looked down and said, 'He's not a rocket scientist. Let's make it real clear what he's to do with his life.' And they allowed me to be raised in a missionary family in a poverty-stricken village in the Ivory Coast of West Africa.

I was just one of the kids in the village: I ran around, I hunted, I fished, I worked in the fields just like all the other children. The only difference between me and everybody else was the colour of my skin, which was my biggest nemesis. I used to pray every night, 'Please, Lord, if you love me, let me wake up black like all of my friends.'

They taught me everything that I consider really important. All of my values were formed in that place. They taught me about love and joy, hope, courage, and time being your servant not your master. They taught me about strength—that God made you strong not for you, but for you to be there for those who are weak.

I came to America when I was fifteen years old. The first American I met was a taxi driver in Manhattan. This man, in the fifteen-minute ride from the airport to the apartment where we were staying, just about undid all of the values that that village had poured into me. Time was everything to him—apparently it mattered a whole lot whether that light was red or green. I learned later that he wasn't waving to people—that was a gesture of anger that he was using out the window! I was shocked and all I wanted to do was get out of this country called America and get back to my home in Africa. There it was calm, it was peaceful. We were people-oriented in Africa, and the United States was just about as opposite as you could get.

One of the descriptions you give in the book is that African children don't have 'work time' or 'study time' or 'play time'. They play as they work alongside their parents—it's all integrated.

The flow from childhood to adulthood is a natural, smooth flow in settings like my village. The tiniest ones worked right alongside the big ones, except the work was play. They were gathering little twigs while the parents had machetes chopping large pieces of wood for the fire. We added to the value of the family to the extent that we had the ability to. By the time we were fifteen years old, most of my friends and I were fully trained to be African peasant farmers, hunters, fishermen; we knew everything we needed to be fully fledged members of that society.

I love the description you give of how Coca Cola came to your village.

Well, there was a great marketing scheme! We got to 120°F on any given day in that village, and some smart guy in a capital city said, 'You know what? They need to drink this stuff.'

Our village was a tiny, dusty little outpost. One truck came through each week. Our gas station was just a grass hut and a 55-gallon drum at the side of the road. And five crates of Coke get delivered there. The gas attendant had never seen this product, and after he had stacked it up in his hut for a while, he came and asked my father to come and explain what it was. 'I don't even know which hole in the engine I'm supposed to pour it into,' he said. My dad told him that in the United States this was something we drank. They were all so hot, so dad took the bottle opener on his knife and opened one up. Well, the thing fizzed and splattered everywhere, and everybody screamed and ran away!

They never would've seen a drink do that.
No way. All they ever had was water. So my dad told them it was good, took a sip to prove it, and offered it around. One of the guys took a sip and jumped back. 'It bites! It bites like a snake!' My father said that we'd buy the Coke whenever it came through. We were the only ones who drank it.

In the book you talk about how you would like to see children freed from time pressure and hurry, materialism, corrosive competition and fear. I'm interested in that term 'corrosive competition'. How was competition different growing up in Africa?
Well, believe it or not, we played soccer. We played it in our village, frankly, with *no* competition. First of all, we didn't have a ball. We used a piece of chicken! Deep inside a chicken is a sort of bladder, and if you blow it up it will dry in the sun and becomes like a ball. Secondly, everybody played. The field was anywhere the ball went. Women would jump up and kick at it for a while and then go back to their cooking pots. It wasn't about who could score the most points; it was how well we could manage this ball. If anybody fell and got hurt, the game stopped. We would sit and cry with them. I learned later that it's called compassion. You suffer with them.

Then I was sent off to boarding school and there I learned that only twenty-two people got to play, even if there were eighty who wanted to play. Only the best got to play. There were lines that we had to play inside. You couldn't let the ball go outside the line and you can't trust each other's word whether it did or didn't—you had to have a referee. It was all about me getting more scores than you so that I was happy and you were sad. If somebody fell down and got hurt, you didn't stop and help him. You dribbled round him and scored. Then you became the hero.

There is a place for competition in the world, but it isn't competition at the expense of another person's loss. World-class athletes understand that competition at its very best isn't really about anyone else's performance but about their own—how well they do according to their training and their plan. They rarely denigrate the competition; they rarely blame the referees. It's about excellence. In the Bible the apostle Paul talks about running 'the race of faith', but he doesn't talk about beating anyone. He talks about running our own race.

I don't know how bad it is in Australia, but in the States the ugliest place in town is the baseball park and the soccer fields, where the children play and the parents scream at their children to score, score, score. There are kids crying, kids laughing, kids boasting, kids depressed. Too much importance on trophies, winning and losing absolutely sucks the joy out of sport.

Apart from kindness, generosity and compassion, what strategic reasons are there to become champions of the world's children?
First of all, half of all humanity is children. Half of the world right now is under the age of about fifteen, and they're the poorest half of the world. When things go wrong in society children pay the greatest price. When there is famine, adults get hungry but it's the children who starve. When there is disease, adults get sick but little ones die. More children have been killed in the last ten years' worth of wars than soldiers. Our ugliest sins like pornography become child pornography or child prostitution. And, by the way, child pornography and prostitution doesn't actually exist—that's really called child rape.

One of the first things we do with children is teach them how to stand in line in school—how to queue up. The tragedy in our world is that they are always at the end of the line. They have no voice. They don't vote. Every element of society has learned how to lobby and protest on behalf of their own agenda, but not children. Have you ever been to a children's protest? I don't think so. Have you ever seen the children's hall of fame? They don't know how to give plaques to mobilise people to champion their cause. They don't have any money to give them. The only money kids have is hugs.

But those of us who believe in children realise—and Proverbs 31:8 says it very clearly—that we must speak up for those who can't speak up for themselves. Frankly, none of us need another day of education about this. We are all child development experts. Most of us spent eighteen years as a child; we deserve honorary PhDs in this field. And I argue that those of us who have been through childhood need to look back at the next generation and ask what we can do to lift them up. What can we do to remove the barriers that keep them from understanding God's love, or keep them from understanding how precious they are, or keep them from recognising the potential that God put in them. We must speak for those who can't speak for themselves.

Wess, there is one chapter in the book that I could hardly get through because of what you describe. Your upbringing in Africa, as wonderful as it was, had a negative side. You were sent to a denominationally-run boarding school and there you were terribly abused. It's quite ironic: today you lead an international organisation focused on helping children, but as a child you held your sick African friends as they died, and you suffered abuse at the hands of your American teachers. How have those experiences changed you?
Well, you know, I can look back on it now and I can see the perfect tapestry—that God had his hand in this. I understand poverty like

very few people who lead these organisations, because I didn't just get a PhD in this field, I've lived it. I lost little friends to what I later discovered was poverty. They didn't need to die. And you're right—some of them died right in my arms.

Every year of my childhood was split between this incredibly loving poverty-stricken village that built my spirit and soul, and a boarding school where all of us missionary kids from West Africa were sent. It was mission policy for us to go to the boarding school. There was no alternative; our parents didn't make these decisions.

It was far from home. We didn't see our parents for nine months at a time. The people who were running this school didn't want to be. They had gone to Africa to be missionaries—to win people for Christ. They didn't make it linguistically, culturally or something. They weren't fired but given the lowest priority job you could have: if they couldn't do this 'missionary stuff', at least they could take care of the missionary kids.

There were eighty of us children in that place. We were under the dominion, if you will, of people who first of all were not *called* to work with children, were not *trained* to minister to children, and who did not *want* to minister to children. We were abused every way that children could be abused. We were abused spiritually— scared to death of God and his judgment on our lives. We were abused emotionally—I was a wreck as a six-year-old boy. I barely talked; I mumbled. I barely wrote; my letters all ran together. And the reason for all of that is I didn't think anybody would care what I had to say or what I thought.

We were beaten with either a belt or a truck tyre-tread slipper. I was beaten many times a day. Spiritually, emotionally, physically we were beaten and abused year after year. Probably the most diabolical part of all this was that we didn't get to tell our parents.

We wrote letters every week but we never told them about the horrors we were going through. The teachers warned us that if we told our parents we would be Satan's tool to destroy their ministry. They used to say, 'There will be Africans in hell because of you if you tell your parents what is happening.'

Diabolical.
They used our love for God, our love for our parents and our love for Africans to silence us about what was going on, which should've landed them in prison. I didn't talk about this until I wrote *Too Small to Ignore*. Almost forty years have gone by. If you had asked me five years ago about my life I would've told you about the village, but I never would've gone into this because I felt I'd have to apologise for God for not taking care of little Wesley.

But as I stepped back and wrote the book I realised I was looking at the wrong side of the tapestry. I was looking at the knots and the tangles. I then recognised that God had made me to be a champion for children. I looked at the other side of the tapestry and thought, Oh my word, I needed to understand poverty and I needed to have felt abuse in order to speak out about all of the ways that children are destroyed.

Poverty and abuse say the same message to a child—give up. Nobody believes in you. There is nobody coming on a white horse to rescue you. Nothing is special about you. Give up. That's a message straight from the gates of hell. That is Satan's message to try and destroy people.

So by God's grace I'm alive, and by God's grace I'm of some use in his kingdom, and I can now realise it was all part of God's plan. After I had been beaten I would go scream into my pillow as a six and seven-year-old boy: 'God, please have mercy on me, have mercy.' I'm sure that my guardian angel went to the Lord and said, 'Do you not hear this?' And now I understand that God must have said, 'I hear every cry, I see every tear, but he needs this. I am shaping this man's heart to one day champion children just like himself.'

Today your heart must break every time you see a child who is still in poverty, who is waiting for that hand up from somebody else. Because you don't just know about poverty and hardship, you've felt it.
These are not statistics to me. I know thirty thousand children die every day of things we can prevent. I know that information. But it goes way beyond statistics for me. I know their names; I know what they look like; they were my boyhood friends. I even know *who* dies. Good ones die. I had friends who gave away their food and gave away their malaria medicine to other little children in their last days thinking those children needed it more than they did. And they're the ones that died.

Heaven is going to be a wonderful place because far better people than us are already there waiting for us.

Duncan Armstrong

THE FUTURE IS TAKEN CARE OF

Raised in the Central Queensland town of Rockhampton, Duncan Armstrong rose to national and international fame at the Seoul Olympics in 1988 when he broke the world record to win the Gold medal in the 200 metres freestyle. Duncan formed a winning relationship with madcap coach Laurie Lawrence which spanned ten years, collecting Gold at the Commonwealth Games, Pan Pacific Championships and numerous national and international competitions.

After representing Australia at two Olympic Games, Duncan retired from the pool in 1993 to pursue a career in media and corporate coaching. During an Easter interview a couple of years back, he recounted how his life had recently taken an unexpected spiritual turn.

You retired from pro swimming in 1993; it just doesn't seem that long ago.
Yeah, many, many moons ago at the age of twenty-five. I'd been swimming for about nine years at the top level and that was it for me. I pulled the pin in '93 after the Pan Pacs. I had a great career. I had a really fun time, met a lot of good people, got to visit a lot of different countries and really climbed to the top of my sport.

Going back, did you always want to swim?
Yeah, pretty much. I grew up in Rockhampton and the temperature up there meant that if you were around a swimming pool you escaped the heat. So I grew up only ever wanting to swim. I met some great people who taught me how to swim and then I met some great coaches who encouraged me and fixed my style. I was always determined to go to the Olympic Games and got there when I was twenty. I always consider myself one of the lucky ones because I was never confused about what I wanted to do.

Is the career path of an Olympic Gold medallist a career path you would recommend, so to speak?
Absolutely; if that's where your drive and determination is. It's one of those wonderful things that very few people get to do, so it's a pretty exclusive club, and there are some wonderful sports to take part in as an Olympian. It really is a great career path in Australia because as a sportsman here you get recognised a great deal. You get a lot of opportunities come your way, and we seem to be sitting right up there above politicians and dentists for popularity! So finding a career in sport, one of the Olympic sports, especially, is a wonderful thing to do in Australia.

What have you learnt from swimming that isn't swimming-related? What else did it teach you?
It taught me a great deal about commitment, time management, self-control and how to get out of bed early in the morning. It taught me how to deal with people, how to be a mentor, how to be mentored, how to be a leader, how to be a follower, how to be part of a team and also lead your own career. So those sort of things have always kept me in good stead whatever I've done business-wise—media

commentary, starting my own business, stuff like that outside of swimming—and helped the way my character has been developed.

What activities mainly take your time these days?
I do three or four things. I've got my own business in the performance area—helping corporations with motivation and direction for their staff. I help out some charities. I do television and radio commentary for a couple of media outlets. I do a little bit of writing and a bit of personal training. All up it leads to a very, very busy life. And I've got two beautiful sons and now a beautiful daughter and I have an amazing wife, so they are my focus and my motivation. That's why I work so hard.

Do you miss competitive swimming?
I used to. I missed it for about four or five years after retirement. It made me very bitter and twisted on the inside. I always felt that I was better than the people running around or swimming. It wasn't until I was able to put a lot of those devils to rest that I really started to grow as a person. Now I thoroughly enjoy it as a spectator and a commentator. I have no desires whatsoever to do any of that strenuous exercise or go under the pressure of competition again. So I can really, really appreciate it now. It wasn't always that way.

A couple of years ago you and your wife found yourself in a church. What led to that?
We had some very strong friends who were Christians and my mate lived his life the way I wanted to live my life. But he had this very interesting strength about him. It was through the power of witnessing his faith and his walk that we ended up in church, and Jesus was ready to crash tackle us and get us into a headlock, and that was the end of that! It really was like a light going on.

For my wife and I, it was the start of our real life. We have been very, very committed to getting to know Jesus, to following his teachings and his ways, being part of our church and now hopefully witnessing to others by the way we hold ourselves and the integrity we live by. We are very committed to being crazy Christians, my wife and I. And we are committed to raising crazy Christian kids. Everyone sort of cringes at that, but we—as brand new Christians—think that is quite real. If someone thinks I'm a crazy Christian then I'm getting it right.

Absolutely. They've just paid you a wonderful compliment.
I think so.

Was it during those turbulent years after professional swimming that you began thinking about spiritual things?
Oh no, no, no—those years were me going though a second adolescence. Those years were me being completely awful to myself and everybody around me; thinking that I needed to be seen, having an identity problem. I look back at those years now as a tremendous growing experience, but boy oh boy, I was unhappy. I was just getting into all kinds of trouble and mischief.

It wasn't really until I started to settle down, and really looked at my relationship with Beckie and my relationship with my sons, that I could really see how far away from the good stuff I was. It wasn't until I calmed down that I could actually open my heart to God—that he could enter it and make a profound change.

Tell me about that first visit to church. What was it like? Did it confirm your image of church, blow it away, or what?
I didn't really have an opinion of church. We didn't grow up in a religious family. If anything I had a bit of prejudice from, you

know, reading all the crusader stories—how bad the church has been in the past; how people want to highlight the bad things but not the good things. I was, like everybody else, very self-reliant. I thought I had it all worked out.

I'd never worshipped before and I'd never seen anyone singing before. We went to an Assemblies of God church which were all a bunch of happy clappers—everyone clapping, cheering and yelling, just having a whale of a time during the worship. I'd never seen anything like that, and I started reading the words and listening to it. For me it became a very emotional experience. My wife and I just stood there holding hands and having a big cry.

Two or three years down the track now I can still go to my church and cry. I just weep because the goodness of God is just so powerful. I've been asked to come and share my testimony quite a few times but I just can't do it. I start out talking about how we came to God and then I start crying. I don't weep, I blubber! I've written it out and I'm a public speaker by trade, so I don't know what is going on. It doesn't upset me; it just freaks me out, because I've got something to say, I want to tell people about my faith, I've got something to share, I want to make an impact on blokes out there who are un-churched, but I just can't get to it! So that is where Jesus has got me at the moment [in] talking about my relationship with him; he has got me at such an emotional point that I'm not there yet. I just cry at the podium every time I talk about it.

It sounds like your Christian conversion has touched you from the inside out. How did that work itself out in the rest of your life—your relationship with your wife and others?
We became a lot more real. Our relationship was good in terms of what the world thinks, but in our hearts we probably weren't all

there—we both admit that. We were having thoughts and doing things that made no sense whatsoever when you look at how we relate now. That is what the Bible has delivered. The Bible has delivered for us a blueprint on how to treat each other, and therefore how to be in a marriage together—the trust and the hedging—and that flows out to the way we treat people around us.

That meant some argy-bargy with some members of our group and families. Some of those people we're estranged from, and that is the hard part. We have confidence that it will get better, and we pray a great deal that the friendships and the family that we don't see any more we will eventually come back to have an authentic relationship with. But at the moment that is not possible with how we are living our life through our relationship with God. While some of it has just been so wonderful, some of it has been sad.

I was going to ask you what the reaction had been to your newfound faith from your family, friends and colleagues . . .
The people who really know us can see a complete change, because when you become a Christian there is a massive amount of re-invention going on. Jesus is busily renovating your heart. As your actions soften or change and people see a different pattern coming in, some get freaked out and others are happy for you. We've had our fair share of that. It's been polarising to say the least.

So, it's only been a couple of years since that dramatic life-changing event took place. That means this is only your second or third Easter. How is Easter different for you now?
It means a great deal more. I'm still reading about it. It's funny: as Easter and Christmas and other biblical events come up through

the year, you seem to get more educated about it and see the meaning within it. Every year the re-invention continues because you never stop getting to know Jesus, so every year you're different coming up to Easter. The resurrection is the really important thing, for me.

I own *The Passion of the Christ* and I watch it regularly because it humbles me to see the effort that Jesus put in for me and for everybody around me. That's what Easter is about for me; it's a humbling experience that centres me. It is truly a gift, to tell you the truth. You can focus on the overwhelming relationship God has with us, each and every one of us, which is quite unbelievable, and then he's got time to make the world the way it is. It's pretty good stuff, I'm telling you.

Duncan, where do you think you are going to be in ten years' time? What are the plans?
To tell you the truth, the future is taken care of for us. We try to live as much as possible knowing that we have a loving God on our side and that he wants the best for us. So we've just got to attune ourselves to his wishes and his guidance, keep on praying and humbling ourselves, throwing ourselves down in front of him, and our future is guaranteed.

I'm not too sure what the future holds. I'm going to be doing media still, and I'm going to keep doing my performance training with a colleague in Brisbane, which I love. The exciting part is I'm going to Bible college. My wife is more of a feeling person and I'm the know-it-all of the family. I have to know stats and motivations and all these sort of things, and I think Bible college will help me out on that.

Could you see yourself doing Christian work in a greater capacity then?
Absolutely. I have been in touch with some great pastors in Brisbane

already. I attend Brisbane City Church and they have got this fantastic giving arm called City Care, and they are working with the down-and-outs in Brisbane; people badly affected by drugs, abuse, alcoholism and stuff like that—people who need our help. So I think my ultimate path will be doing charity somewhere.

Again the Bible college stuff comes back into it, because the Bible connects me to people 2000 years ago and to people thousands of years before that. You know, normal people like you and me with real emotions, but it's all in the Bible. I find myself so many times within the Bible with people like Noah, Jonah, Nehemiah and all these sorts, thinking, I am like them. So the Bible connects me to people from the dawn of time and I'd like to know more about them.

Could we see you as a church pastor at some stage?
I don't know. If God calls and that is the job for me, I don't mind. I think it freaks my wife out a little bit because we see the pastor's job as so consuming; a very, very responsible and dedicated position. So at this stage, only being in the faith for five minutes, we have a lot of work to do if that ever happens. But you never know. Maybe in ten or fifteen years' time when we have more of a grip on the whole deal, it might be where he calls us.

FAITH

The great paradox of the 21st century is that, in this age of powerful technology, the biggest problems we face internationally are problems of the human soul.
Ralph Peters

Take your everyday, ordinary life—your sleeping, eating, going-to-work, and walking-around life—and place it before God as an offering.
Saint Paul

Eugene Peterson

Eugene Peterson has spent nearly five decades providing spiritual guidance to a worldwide audience through his twenty five-plus books. He is best known for his paraphrase of the Bible called *The Message*, which today is read by over ten million people.

When told that Bono was quoting *The Message* at U2 concerts Peterson replied, 'Who's Bono?' Hip he isn't, but that could well be why Eugene Peterson has had such an impact on so many.

I take it you now know who Bono is?
I do know who Bono is.

It came as quite a surprise to you, I believe, that he was quoting The Message *in front of 20,000 fans at a time.*
Yeah, it did come as a surprise. My students, who all love Bono and U2, quickly re-educated me!

After forty-five years as a church minister and scholar, you are now officially retired. Does that really mean anything? You're still churning out books.
Well, it means something, but it doesn't mean that I'm not working as hard as I ever did. I just spent two days with a group of camp

85

directors from all over the country in a retreat place just a mile from our house. So most of the people come to me now—I don't go to them.

The Message *has been so popular, hasn't it?*
It's just astonishing. I had no idea that would be the case.

Why do think it has resonated with us so much?
You know, Sheridan, I really don't know. I had no idea that I was doing anything extraordinary. I have been doing this all my life in my congregation—a very small congregation. Nobody thought it was so great there. Somehow it has caught the imagination. I was trying to get [the Bible's message] into the colloquial language that I was listening to all my life—with my congregation, my kids, the neighbourhood—and it just struck fire somehow.

Is it true that you assembled The Message *from Bible study notes you'd written over the years for your congregation?*
Yes. I was thinking of these new Christians, and Christians who had got tired of reading the Bible, who thought they knew it all. So I was trying to wake them up to what was going on there. And they woke up.

It must have been quite a weight on your shoulders to actually translate the Scriptures. If I was in that role part of me would be thinking, 'Well, I hope I get this right. I don't want to lead people astray.'
Well, Sheridan, it wasn't quite like that. I had scholars who would check what I did. For every book of the Bible there was an evangelical scholar who had written a commentary on that book and I would submit it to him or her. So I felt I had a safety net, so that they

could find inadvertent mistakes or things that would cause some shade of mishearing or mis-meaning in the text. I felt very light, actually. I felt very joyful. It was a twelve-year project, and to tell you the truth I never did get tired of it.

Let's go back a few years. Your early years were spent in your father's butcher shop in Montana. Did that apprenticeship of sorts provide any basis for the spiritual apprenticeship you would later offer to others?
Yes, it did. In fact, it might have been the most important influence on my life as a pastor.

My father was a butcher, wore a white apron, and my mother, when I was about five years old, started making little white aprons for me. I would work in his butcher shop. Well, work—I was there and messed around. But I was gradually given jobs to do. And I knew the story of Samuel, whose mother made him a priestly robe, and I pretended that I was Samuel and my father was a priest. In fact, my father acted like a priest. He knew everybody who came into the store by name. He was an affable, cheerful, relational person. And of course we were in a place of sacrifice—we were killing chickens, goats and lambs. So I felt quite at home, and I realised later when I became a pastor how much influence that place of exchange had on me. My father's priestly presence was very important.

Would you say he was the greatest spiritual influence in your life?
Yeah, together with my mother. My home was the nurturing place for my vocation. My mother was a great storyteller and so her love for words, stories, her language—that was in my genes from her. But this other kind of public presence of personal and relational care of people, making sure they were getting what they needed, that came from my father.

How did your faith journey begin? When was the moment when God became real to you?

That's hard to say when you grow up in a world where everything is so congruent and fits together. My whole world was the world of faith. There was an outside world, but I wasn't much part of that. But I had moments of realisation during conversations with my parents. I saved up money and brought my first Bible when I was twelve. The Psalms became very important to me at any early age. So I started praying the Psalms when I was about twelve, thirteen or fourteen and have done it ever since. It's been the basic text for my life of prayer. I think I have probably written about the Psalms more than any other single part of the Scripture.

What disciplines and practices do you undertake to maintain your relationship with God? Are you comfortable exploring that with us?

Yeah I am, but I guess I'm a little bit reluctant—I don't want anybody copying me. They should be doing it themselves. But, you know, I'll tell you what I do. I have been doing this as long as I've been an adult and previous to that, actually. I get up early in the morning and I have an hour-and-a-half or two hours which starts with a mug of coffee. I grind my beans and steep my coffee and take a flask of it to my wife and go to my study.

To tell you the truth, Sheridan, I really don't think of that time as devotional time. I'm praying, I'm reading the Bible, I'm meditating; I'm just trying to be present before God. But when I leave my study, that's when I begin. I feel like [that morning time] is the stretching and callisthenics you do before you run a race. Then you're into the world and you're praying. That's when the praying starts—grappling with life in Jesus' name.

If there was one deliberate thing I've done that has made more difference to me than anything else—to my wife, to my family, to my congregation, to my children—it's been keeping a Sabbath. We started to keep the Sabbath when our children were young. I worked hard on Sunday, of course, so that couldn't be my Sabbath. So we took Monday for our Sabbath. We kept it pretty strict. Except for emergencies like deaths and accidents, we didn't do any work activities. We asked the congregation to help us do it, and they did. We defined our Sabbath as 'play and pray'—we didn't do anything necessary. We usually started it by going to the woods and spending five or six hours walking along the rivers and through the woods, not with a Bible but with binoculars. We spent the first three or four hours in silence, had lunch together, then talked on our way back home. When we got home the kids would be coming home from school and we would just play. And we've done that for forty years. I think in terms of deciding to do something and keeping a deliberate practice, that has probably been the most significant thing we have done.

A Sabbath puts the handbrake on this hectic life of ours, doesn't it?
Yeah. It just says stop, quit. Watch what God is doing for a while, just today. Just watch what he is doing. He is watching what you are doing for six days—it's pretty generous of him. So just watch what he is doing. Listen to what he is saying.

How can we watch what God is doing? Where do you think the signs of his presence are in the world?
Well, we've got a pretty good text book to know what to look for. We read Scripture with a kind of attentiveness, and we listen to people in a different way—listening to the meaning beneath their words or within their words. People around us are great carriers of God's presence, whether they know it or not.

One of the things I regret among my fellow friends and neighbours is that we really don't take Scripture seriously, personally, and read it as attentively as we do the newspapers. What's going on? I live out in the country. I walk twenty minutes to get the morning newspaper. But I've spent an hour-and-a-half or two hours by that time trying to pay attention to what God is doing as revealed in Jesus, in the Scriptures. I get my paper, open it up, and I look at the front page and see what the editor thought was important for me to know. It takes me about five minutes and I've had enough. There is nothing new in that newspaper. Every day there are murders, rapes or drug deals; there is almost never anything new. But when I open my Bible, you know, I'm surprised every day. Why didn't I ever see that before? Even evangelicals, who read the Bible every day, are not paying attention to it.

I wonder if this relates back to a statement of yours I read once, that spirituality is in a mess today. How do you think spirituality needs to be reformed?

That is hard to say. I have written twenty-five books or so trying to address that topic.

I'll tell you what I think I know about what's gone wrong. We have been so taken by the secularised world, the celebrity world, the world of addictions, of stimulus, of adrenalin—we have brought into that whole thing. For instance, I can't believe that everybody has a television set in their home. Why do they do that? Who wants all that poison coming into your house? The addiction to the internet. The haste—everybody is in a hurry. Why do they do that? Doesn't anybody want to learn how to live simply?

I was in a monastery a few years ago and there were thirty or forty people making retreat there, and the guest master gathered all of us together and said, 'If there is anything you need, come and see us. We will tell you how you can do without it.' I've been trying to do that as a pastor for all my adult life but, you know, that is not a very popular way to be a pastor.

After a lifetime of walking with God, what one aspect of the person of Jesus most captivates you today?

His absolute embrace of ordinary stuff, and ordinary people. He wasn't going after the big people in his day. He ignored them. He went after the little people, the outsiders, the bystanders. I'm writing right now about the way we use languages. I'm just immersed in the parables, the way Jesus talked and how he was able to enter into the ordinary lives of people who didn't even care about God, didn't know about God, weren't interested in God. And suddenly by entering into their life using their language, not importing a spiritual high-powered language into their lives, he gently got into their lives and then they got into his life. He is the word made flesh, and language becomes such an important way in which he communicates, creates, heals. Your question is what most impresses me. That's what impresses me. That presence. His speaking presence.

Andrew Denton

So one of Australia's best-known TV personalities decides to do a documentary on American evangelical Christianity. How would it turn out? Would stereotypes of wacky televangelists prevail? And why would this high-profile host want to make such a film in the first place?

For four days in February 2006, *Enough Rope* presenter Andrew Denton conducted interviews at the 63rd National Religious Broadcasters conference in Texas. The result was a documentary called *God On My Side*. I asked Denton what prompted his film, and how he might describe his own beliefs on matters spiritual.

Why do a documentary like this? When did the idea first come to mind?
Last year a friend sent me an article about the convention of the National Religious Broadcasters, and it just fascinated me. I thought, what an amazing group of people, and what an opportunity to look at George Bush's America but not through the obvious window of politics, but through faith, because 40% of his vote are evangelical Christians.

I was particularly fascinated by one detail in the article about the fact that the largest display at this Christian convention was for the Israeli Tourism Bureau, and the centrepiece of their display was a bus they had flown over from Jerusalem which had been blown up by a suicide bomber in which a number of people had died. I was really intrigued as to what kind of people that would be a tourist attraction for, and why.

Did you ever get the answer to that? It wasn't actually on display when you went to this convention, was it?
That's right; it was a much more straightforward display.

Look, the answer lies in a very literal Old Testament view, an end-times view of the world which says—and many people I spoke to at the convention believed this—that for Jesus to return to earth, for the rapture to happen, for the taking up of Christians into the arms of the Lord, it is biblically mandated that Israel must be in the hands of the Jews, and therefore it is a biblical duty for Christian Americans who believe this to support the nation state of Israel, regardless. That means also, I think, regardless of a two-state solution.

As you were walking around the convention doing these interviews with various promoters, what surprised you?
One thing that surprised me was how readily and universally people agreed when I asked the question, 'Is George Bush God's man at this hour?' It is one thing to say you support him politically, but it's a much stronger thing to say that he's God's man at this hour. So I was very surprised at that clear and direct connection between faith and politics.

Was there anything that unsettled you?
Frankly, Sheridan, I'm always unsettled by people with absolute beliefs—people who basically say there is only one truth, I know

what it is, and ultimately if you don't agree with it you've got it coming to you. I find that unsettling. It doesn't matter what the religion is.

I must admit that as I was watching the documentary, I did squirm a little bit at the extent to which the word 'Christian' is as much a brand name in some quarters as it is a faith. Did that make any impression on you?

Look, first and foremost this is a convention of people whose job it is to market the word of Christianity—which is a perfectly appropriate thing for them to be doing. But the business model was no different, I suspect, to any large convention of any large business. So you had everything from Christian television stations through to people selling Christian lollipops. One of our interviewees, a filmmaker, disapproves in fact [of] all the 'goofy Jesus trinkets'. It's no great news, and no great surprise—but nonetheless fascinating to see—that in America Christian broadcasting and the industry around it is very, very big business.

After watching a preview of God On My Side *I asked the person sitting next me what question they would like to ask you. They said, 'Ask him why he didn't interview any normal people'! You recorded these interviews at a broadcasters conference with promoters at stands selling all manner of wares. Could it be that you got the views of, not American evangelicals as such, but American evangelical salespeople?*

No, I think it was a whole range of people. I would actually disagree that they're not normal people. I think they are very representative of George Bush's America and that's why we went there, because here was a large collection of 6000 people from all walks of life and with many different businesses, some big and some very small.

We could have told a different story and could have made a different documentary. You said in your introduction about the televangelists. We could have painted that extreme picture, but we went out of our way to speak to what I view as, if you like, the foot soldiers of George Bush's heartland. Half the people we lined up beforehand and half the people we met there on the floor. We left ourselves open to the possibility of who we would meet.

I think it's a broad and interesting mix of different views. Not everyone agrees either. I'm sure someone like Phil Cook would take great exception to not being called 'normal'. He is a liberal Christian with a very liberal Christian view of the world, and doesn't approve of the conservative Christians, saying that for too long 'we've been against things rather than for them'. So I actually think there is a broad sweep of views there and, with respect, take issue with them not being 'normal'.

I guess you're still dealing with predominantly salespeople rather than the average person in the pew though.
But they are also average people in the pew. It's like saying, 'Why speak to a businessman about his belief when you could be speaking to somebody in the street?' Faith is not about what you do for a living; faith is about how you view the universe and that is what ties these people together. The fact that some of them are broadcasters, or scriptwriters, or in the case of the MacDuff Brothers, actual pastors—it just happens to be what they do. It doesn't determine how they see the world.

I think you handled the documentary fairly, and I didn't see any ridiculing—which I was wondering if we'd have, given the subject matter.

You know what? It would've been really wrong to do that. It would have been wrong professionally—this film is not meant to be about what I think. But secondly, I didn't believe that personally. I don't agree with all those views in the film, but I have great respect for people's individual faith.

It's not for me to tell anyone that their faith is wrong, or to mock either. I think faith is the fundamental personal question. What is the universe? Why are we here? What are we here for? I respect everybody's journey to that. When faith is then tied to the machinery of state or the machinery of war or the machinery of society, and where somebody's faith tells them to tell someone else that they can't live a certain way—that's when I think questions need to be asked.

Some would say, 'Well, couldn't there have been room for more moderate evangelical leaders to be interviewed—say, a Bill Hybels or a Eugene Peterson or a Jim Wallis? Were those kinds of people sought out for the documentary at all?

Well, those kinds of people weren't there. We restricted it to who was at the convention. We did have an interview lined up with Pastor Jack Graham, and an interview lined up with Frank Wright—the President of the NRB—and both of those were cancelled by them, without reason given to us. Certainly through Phil Cook and Brian Godawa, who represent a more liberal Christian view of the world, we did set out to speak to a range of voices.

I'm certainly not claiming that this is a total view of the Christian world but it is representative of what we found at that convention. That convention is the heartland of George Bush's evangelical Christian America. They are 40% of his vote and that's why we thought it was a relevant group of people to talk to.

You can say of any film, it was about *this* but why wasn't it about *that*? Well, it wasn't about *that* because it was about *this*.

I will be interested to see what the average Australian thinks of Australian evangelicals after watching God On My Side. *Do you think there could be transference from what they see there to what they see here? In what way?*

Well, in the sense that Australia follows America a fair bit, so that's what Australian evangelicals must be like too.
Look, there may be some of that. In the end that's the thing about faith. It's an invisible, isn't it? You can't see it. It can go everywhere.

But America and Australia have different histories. America has a far stronger religious core to its history than Australia does. It's the country where fundamentalism basically started. I think we have a different nature. But there is nothing wrong with people holding a fundamentalist Christian view; there is no reason why Australians couldn't hold that view as well. I'm not sure that this film will necessarily be the *cause* for others to take it up.

Andrew, I would love to know how you describe yourself religiously or spiritually.
Extremely doubtful! I went to a Jewish kindergarten, a Catholic primary school and a Church of England secondary school.

You're confused!
Absolutely! And I came away not subscribing to any of it. But I don't say that defiantly or boastfully, in that, as I said, these are fundamentally personal questions. My lack of belief gets down to just a core feeling—I don't have any sense of 'the Other'. I admit

to some suspicion about organised religion, even though it can be a great force for good and through many individuals is. It is equally and historically a great force for destruction. In many cases religion is politics by other means. So I cock an eye, I suppose, at organised religion and its excesses on occasions.

But my personal view is I don't have belief in God. But would I say that's the right answer? No, like everybody else I'm still looking.

Did your time talking with the folks at the National Religious Broadcasters conference encourage or dampen any of those, I guess, latent feelings? Did it confirm your current doubt? I guess what I would love to know is, as you were wandering around the exhibits, were you led at all to question if there was something to it?

No, I wasn't stirred in that way. But what it did do is it made me far more strongly interested in the Bible and where it has come from. Pastor Doug Batchelor, who is the 'end times' pastor—I had a couple of chats to him and it was just fascinating. I had been reading Deuteronomy—some incredibly punitive passages about what is going to happen to the enemies of the Lord—and I asked him, 'Who wrote that?' He said, 'Well, that was Moses' last testament, his last writing.' I was really interested in the history of where this was coming from.

I guess a general answer to your question is that I came away from the convention even more curious about faith and why a person's faith drives them where it does. It's really interesting to me. It's almost like the very heart of the human condition. Did it actually stir a greater sense of faith in me? No. But it absolutely stirred a greater curiosity in the question *of* faith.

Was the person of Jesus there to be seen or was he smothered under all the products?
No, he was there. I don't think anyone should believe for a second that this was just a business convention. I think we say in the film that people go to network and to sell things, but it's also about being inspired. There is a genuine and deep belief among these people. I don't think I met anyone who I would say was in any way just doing it for the money, or being hypocritical.

You know, as I've just told you, I don't have a belief in God. It would be lovely to have that depth of faith; it would be lovely to have that sense of sureness about the universe. I have a real respect for the journeys these people have made. It did strike me, though, and I say this in the film, that a number of these people had come to God through great trauma. I'm curious about that; whether the depth of faith was partly caused by the depth of pain.

Could we see any similar documentaries of this kind in the future from you?
Maybe. As I've said, it's a subject which I think is really interesting. And I think what religion does to people and what people do to religion is one of the great stories of history. I feel like I have only just touched the surface really.

Finally, Andrew Denton, you're the man behind David Tench Tonight, *I believe. I didn't realise that until about a week ago and now I can see a distinct resemblance between the two of you.*
It must be my own God delusion. Here I am creating somebody *not* in my own image.

You end the Enough Rope *program with you pulling on the finger of what seems like a very divine hand.*
It's a nod to Michelangelo more than anything, but yes, that's true. Well, I remember winning divinity prizes when I was in primary school. I was well educated and it's showing my background.

Well educated—still confused!
Oh absolutely! My job is to ask lots of questions. I don't necessarily have lots of answers.

Max Lucado

Max Lucado has touched millions around the world with his signature storytelling writing style. The author of more than fifty books, including *In the Grip of Grace*, *When God Whispers Your Name*, *He Chose the Nails* and *3:16 The Numbers of Hope*, over twenty-eight million copies of Lucado's books are in print today.

The influential *Christianity Today* magazine once called him 'America's Pastor', and *Reader's Digest* once crowned him the best preacher in America. But I have a feeling Max would rather be known simply as a husband, a father and a follower of Jesus. We talked about finding faith, avoiding moral failure and discovering our 'sweet spot' in life.

What would you like to be known as?
A sinner saved by grace. God has been good to me, despite the fact that I had ignored him for many years in my life. So I think, if nothing else, to know that God was kind to me and had mercy upon me even though I ignored him—that would be the greatest legacy I could leave.

Your own path to faith actually had a few bends and kinks in it. Recount that for us.
Well, I developed a pretty serious drinking problem when I was

young. Even though my parents did all they could to direct me onto the right path, I fell in with a crowd. They were stronger than I was.

I have this insatiable appetite for beer, and just one beer is never enough for me. So by the time I was eighteen I realised that I could drink a lot more than my buddies without feeling it. I was developing a tolerance towards alcohol and, quite honestly, I enjoyed that for a while. But it scared me. I wondered where it was going to take me.

At about the age of twenty somebody explained to me about the teachings of God, especially about his son Jesus. I came to believe that Jesus is God's son and when he died on the cross he died so that I could go to heaven. That was authenticated to me as I studied the resurrection. And I realised that if Jesus really rose from the dead then he has authority over my mistakes and my rebellion, and so I received his forgiveness. It's been literally a great life since. I don't battle the alcoholism any longer [although] I have to be careful. And I am finally convinced that he has forgiven me for all those mistakes I made during those years.

If you were to sum it up in a sentence, what would you say is your life message?
I think it would be this: God loves, so God gave; we believe and so we live.

I like that. Spoken by a true preacher!
Remember the most famous verse in the Bible: 'For God so loved the world that he gave his one and only son, so that whoever believes in him will not perish but have eternal life.' You have to keep things simple for me. I'm not the brightest bulb in the drawer.

And that passage makes sense to me. God loves me. I can get my head around that. He gave exactly what I needed—a sacrifice for my sins and mistakes. If I believe, if I just trust that, then life begins within me.

If I could share with any person, in any subway, airplane or situation, it would be that message.

Christianity Today called you America's pastor and Reader's Digest *said you're the best preacher in America. You've probably sold more books than any other Christian author in the world. How do you combat the tempting lure of being a Christian celebrity?*
That is a great question, Sheridan, because sometimes I believe what people say about me. And that is the most dangerous thing to do. You begin thinking, 'I must really be *special.*' But I'm not. I'm really not. I struggle just like everybody else with pride. Pride is the core of sin.

You know, when Adam and Eve were in the garden and the serpent approached Eve and said, 'Did God really say if you eat from this you shall not die?' I think he was playing with her pride, testing her, and saying, 'If you do this you will be like God.' So there is something inside us all that wants to be our own little gods. It's a challenge   it is. I don't always succeed.

Now, God humbles me regularly. Right now, for example, I'm battling a heart condition. I've had fifty-two years of phenomenal health but the last nine months I've had an atrial fibrillation. I thought I was Mr Bullet Proof, that I would never have any health issues. It's a reminder that I am very fragile, just like everyone else. And I think God sends us those reminders to keep us dependent on him.

We really are dependent on his enabling moment by moment, aren't we?
Yes sir. He is faithful. He does watch after us. But he is prone to send difficulties to waken us up to look to him.

We've all seen the horrible effects of the Jimmy Swaggarts, Jim Bakkers and, more recently, the Ted Haggards of the Christian world who have had public moral failures. What kind of safeguards have you put in place to keep you on the straight and narrow?
I do believe [that] of him to who much is given much is required. If somebody is entrusted with the care and teaching of a lot of people—hundreds of thousands, if not millions, of people through books—integrity is very important. People interpret the credibility of God through the credibility of his children.

I try to be very careful. As we're engaging in this phone call, for example, I'm in Seattle, Washington. I live in Texas—I've travelled up here to speak at an event this weekend. And I always have someone who travels with me. I never travel alone. When I speak I don't request an honorarium, but I do request two airplane tickets. I know there is someone checking up or checking in with me. It helps minimise the temptation of wandering around in a strange city and doing something that I would live to regret.

Here in the United States pornography is so rampant that as soon as I check into the hotel room I have to call down to the desk and request they switch the adult films off in my room. I don't trust myself for even five minutes alone with those films. So I have to do things like that, just to be careful.

In your book Cure for the Common Life, *you talk about us finding our 'sweet spot' in life. It's a golfing term, but describe how it can be applied more broadly.*

I believe that every single person has a uniqueness about them—a particular aptitude, bent or strength that is unlike any other person alive or indeed has ever lived. When we discover that uniqueness we discover the reason we were placed on this earth. To try to be anything that I want to be is really impossible. I may want to be a certain mechanic or certain carpenter or certain singer, but if those aren't the skills God gave me, I can want to be one all day long. Desire alone won't do it.

I honour God when I study myself and assess what I do well. When what I want to do and what I do well converge together, there I find my 'sweet spot'.

Would you call it the same as finding one's calling or vocation?
Yes, yes. You know, vocation comes from that Latin word *vocare*, or vocal—'to call'. I believe God has given each one of us a calling. There are many places in the Bible that teach this, and of course there any many psychologists and sociologists who embrace the idea. If we can equip our children, especially, to understand that God has made them in a unique fashion and help them understand what is unique about them, we are doing them such a great favour.

Max, how did you personally discover your calling—the thing in life that you were supposed to do?
I assumed that I would be like my father. We all assume that we will be like whoever raised us—whether it's an uncle or a coach or, more personally, a father or a mother.

My dad was a mechanic. He loved to fix things. The problem was that I couldn't tell a carburettor from a spare tyre. I really wanted to be a mechanic like my dad, but I couldn't. I mean, I would try and it just didn't make sense.

But what I *could* do was read. I loved books. Even though my family was not a family given to a lot of books—there weren't many in our house—I could read books all night long. My father noticed that and he made sure that I had a library card.

I also noticed that I loved to write. While other kids groaned at English assignments, I would get excited. I wouldn't get excited at chemistry assignments, or math assignments.

As you look back over your life, what things have you consistently enjoyed doing and done well? Study your life and read your own story, and assume that there is something unique about you.

Let's unpack that further. You use the acrostic STORY as a tool to help us discover our sweet spot and live an uncommon life. Break that open for us.

I could spend the whole program on it, but I'll try and do it quickly. Strength, Topic, Optimal environment, Relationships, Yes—that's your STORY.

What is your Strength? What is that one thing that you do that you do relatively easily? In fact, Sheridan, there is probably something that you do that is not without challenge, but when you do it you say that it wasn't that hard. It came together pretty quickly. That is your strength. When you catch yourself saying, 'Well, that wasn't very hard; why can't everybody do this?', then you are operating in your strength.

You also have a Topic that fascinates you. It might be nature, it might be numbers, it could be colours. But when you find that one topic—for me it's words and messages—then you're finding your sweet spot.

We all have Optimal environments in which we work. I have a friend who works at a hospital and he loves emergency moments. He is, I guess, an emergency room junky. He is at his best when he has to make a decision within a matter of two or three minutes and it's a life or death decision. Others of us would just panic; we need time and space to be able to process. So what is your optimal environment?

The fourth letter stands for Relationships. Do you work better leading people or following people? As you look back over your life and your successful moments, were you by yourself or were you in a group?

Then the last word is Yes—when you do something and you look up and you clench your fist and say, 'Yes! That was great!' My youngest daughter does that when she cooks. She's eighteen, will prepare a meal, and at the end of it say, 'Oh, that was so much fun.' I cannot comprehend that! I see no enjoyment whatsoever in cooking. But I'm still grateful that she does; and because she does, I eat well!

That's the STORY we all have.

I think of when I had three or four months alone to write a book. It was my optimal environment. I also think of the night we launched this show. I was driving home around two o'clock in the morning after we'd wrapped up the very first show and I was slamming the steering wheel, saying 'Yes, yes, yes!'

Way to go, Sheridan! See, what you are doing is you are being responsive to God's story on your heart. I think there is an assumption sometimes made by Christians that if it's enjoyable then it mustn't be my assignment; that to be a follower of Christ means being miserable. It's just the opposite.

I think of Frederick Buechner's great phrase: 'The place God calls you to is where the world's deep hunger and your deep gladness meet.'

I have read that phrase and underlined it myself. I think it's the great summary of the theme of vocation.

As you mentioned before, you've recently had some issues with your heart. How has that changed your understanding of your own unfolding story?

I've not had any health issues for fifty-two years, my entire life, and all of a sudden I'm being reminded on a regular basis that even if you try to take care of yourself these things happen. So it's a wake-up call to me. It encourages me to focus. I'm fifty-two years old; I figure I have two or three decades left if I can take care of myself. What is the lasting contribution I want to make? This gives me a wonderful opportunity to focus in on that and see if I can do a good job.

So what will be your lasting contribution over the next three decades?

I'm going to do more of what we are doing now: writing, and doing more talking about writing about this message. I will probably do a little more travel. My health is doing better now; I've had some good treatments for my heart and, God willing, I would like to travel and encourage people.

Who has been the greatest influence in your writing life and your shaping of words?

You mentioned Frederick Buechner, who is a wonderful writer. I was introduced to him in the 1970s, if not 1980. Somebody gave me a Frederick Buechner book and I remember being amazed at how he could write so creatively about the Christian faith. So he was an early influence for me.

Later on I began reading Chuck Swindoll's writings. Chuck is a dear friend, a man whom I respect very much. The fact that he is a pastor and a writer inspired me to try and do both.

So those two men have had a good influence on me through the years.

What is your optimal environment for writing? Do you need solitude?
I do. I have to get off by myself and need several hours of uninterrupted time. I am no good at writing for thirty minutes here or sixty minutes there; I need a good five or six hours. After five or six hours my brain cells begin to fizzle and so I have to call it a day. I've heard of those who can go all night long. I don't do that well.

As we speak you're starting to finish a chapter of your life—completing twenty years of service as the Senior Minister of Oak Hills Church in San Antonio, Texas. Did life ever slip into commonness during those years?
Yes, I have battled that. Leading a church can feel like you're just leading a company, an organisation. You have budgets, you have personnel issues, you have property issues, and it begins to take on a corporate feel.

We have to remind ourselves regularly in church that this is an absolutely unique organisation on the face of the earth. The church is the only organisation God calls to pray. He did not call universities or hospitals to be houses of prayer—the church is God's house of prayer. The church is the institution to which God gave his gospel, the promise of eternal life through the death of Christ on the cross. That is a high and holy call that God gives the church so we have to battle against mediocrity as we express those two great gifts.

I want you to leave us with three pieces of advice: one for church leaders, one for aspiring writers and one for those feeling that their life is trapped in the common and the mundane. What would you say to each of those three groups of people?

To church leaders I would say pray and preach Jesus. If we succeed there, great. If we fail there, we fail.

To writers I would say that the secret to good writing is re-writing. Most books could use another draft.

To those whose lives are trapped in the mundane I say listen carefully to the promises of the Bible, like John 3:16—that God so loved the world that he gave his one and only son, that whoever believes in him shall not perish but have eternal life. You are loved by God. Your name is known in heaven. God smiles when he thinks of you and he has an eternal plan, a plan that is beyond this world, beyond this life, for you.

Tim Costello

I love sitting down with folks to discover how they tick. I love delving into their backgrounds to find out how they've become who they've become. How was their character built? What forces shaped them? How did their childhood help or hinder the development of their life's work?

Those are the questions I asked of social campaigner, church leader and World Vision CEO Tim Costello—a man who has done significant things with his energy and talents. The result was an enlightening discussion of faith, justice and discovering one's calling in life.

The name Tim Costello and the phrase 'social justice' go hand in glove. How did that passion for justice develop in you?
Look, it's a funny thing to try and answer that question because what happens to you in family, school and elsewhere is dreadfully normal. You can't necessarily unpick the threads.

I grew up in a family that had a Christian faith, a family that took church attendance and things like Christian Endeavour very, very seriously. I heard stories of missionaries speaking about things that challenged me—people who didn't have what I took for granted, places in the world where they didn't necessarily have the gospel and the good news, or clean water, or access to medicines.

I think that missionary impulse really got me questioning, well, why is the world like this? All of us are made in the image of God. We are all children of God. Why are those of us who are thrown onto the stage of life here in Australia given opportunities, options and choices that others born in Bangladesh and Mozambique aren't? Why even here in Australia are some able to embrace those choices and others end up with mental illness and drug abuse?

So it was, I guess, just the recognition that inequalities and great differences existed, and that forced me to ask those questions. And when you do that, I think a whole journey in social justice is born.

You studied law in university. Could that also be traced back to those early years, hearing those missionaries speak?
Look, that is a curious one. I did my best in the HSC as it was called then (VCE now), without any thought of becoming a lawyer. I must be absolutely frank: law mainly attracted me at that stage because it was a five-year course and I didn't want to work! In fact, after I finished law I still didn't want to work, and so I looked around to stay at university and did another course—a Diploma of Education. Six weeks of teacher training convinced me that law was a very good idea!

Once I got involved in law I saw there was this gap—the gap between what courts deliver and what real justice is; the gap between the rule of law and human rights that get abused. And though law is largely focused on the retributive side (criminal law) or the ordering of society (civil law), it also prompted me to think about the social dimensions of justice: redistributive justice. So like lots of lawyers at Monash I did a course called Poverty Law. Poverty Law back in the 1970s was asking, 'Why is law mainly accessible to those who have got money, and other Australians miss out because they can't pay a lawyer?'

So all of that shaped me too.

Your family is fascinating. Your parents produced a son who would become a church minister, social commentator and campaigner, and another who would become, for many years, the nation's Federal Treasurer. That's quite an accomplishment. What was growing up in that family like?
It was a family that took faith seriously and that took learning seriously. How could it not? Both parents were teachers: one in the private system and one in the state system. Family holidays were extended classrooms. The car drive to Sydney or Adelaide where we would go for holidays in some ways just turned into a private tutorial.

Family meals were always engaging. We'd discuss issues; we would debate what was said in church during the sermon. I remember once, when I was about twelve, one of my friends who came home for Sunday lunch saying, 'Your family is weird. No other family sits and debates like that.' Now, that was normal for us. It wasn't weird. It was, I think, a family where our parents took a hands-on interest in our development and didn't leave education simply to the like of schools and curriculum.

Tim, I'm fascinated with understanding people's sense of call or vocation. And you can't really have a call without a 'Caller'. When did you have a sense that God might be calling you to do something? And has it changed over the years or has it been the one essential calling with different roles?
There have been various layers of call for me. At a young age there

was the call to give my life to Christ. That was the fundamental plank. The notion that God made me was just a staggering notion, as it still is. In my work with Urban Seed, with homeless and drug-affected people, I would say to them, 'Do you know that God made you?' And you would see tears bubble up in their eyes. It's just an astonishing thought.

Then there was for me a strong sense that I was going to do something in Christian ministry. During my first years of university I did a lot of outdoor preaching with a group called Open Air Campaigners. I loved that, and loved engaging evangelistically. I think my skills, and certainly my brother's skills, were honed in some of that outdoor work.

Then there was this sense of call I was talking about earlier, to justice. I became a lawyer; I wanted to make a difference. I wanted to defend those who didn't have access to justice. I eventually set up a branch office of a firm I worked for in St Kilda: a street-front legal office for sex workers, people who had been thrown out of houses because they couldn't afford the rent. For the next decade or more that was my legal practice.

There was a call to building the kingdom of God. That took expression in me being ordained as a Baptist minister at St Kilda Baptist, a small church of about ten members when I started, and to really build that up.

There was a call at one stage to go into local politics. I ended up Mayor of St Kilda, and quoted at my inauguration the words from Isaiah 65: 'They shall build houses and live in them. No longer shall they build houses and others live in them.' So many yuppies had discovered St Kilda, forcing up the rents and forcing out the poor, that I ran on a platform of rate dollars going into affordable housing.

There was a call to found the Urban Seed ministry amongst the homeless and drug affected [of Melbourne]. And, of course, most recently there's been a call to the global stage through World Vision.

So I would have to talk of a number of calls where I have sensed God leading me, saying, 'This is where I want you to be.' And I hope there are more calls to come.

How have those calls come? Has it been through prayer? Have they been dramatic? Or have they been more of a growing 'sense' over a period of time?
They have been, at the time, most undramatic. It's when you look back you actually see God's fingerprints all over them. When I was studying theology in Switzerland we had a call from a number of larger Baptist churches to become the senior minister in the eastern suburbs—the 'Bible Belt' of Melbourne. In fact, Blackburn, where I grew up, was considered the buckle of the Bible Belt. It was known, familiar, safe. But something in me said no. We knew the good news 'worked', if I can put it crudely, in the eastern suburbs. Did the good news work in the inner city, where there was, in the early 1980s, much more poverty, ethnic mix and drug problems? Those urban issues saw churches mainly struggling in the inner city. Something in me just said, no, go for something tougher. And St Kilda eventually approached us when we let it be known we wanted to do something in a small struggling church that couldn't even pay us a stipend, where I had to work to support myself, thus the legal practice.

Was it a call? Looking back, yes. At the time it seemed right to do as we thought about it and prayed. There was no fingerprint of lightning in the sky. Each of my calls I would describe in that way: A sense of niggling. Is this still the right thing to be doing; is this something that I should be open to; am I getting too comfortable? Those have been the ingredients.

What do you understand the 'good news' to be these days?
Well, Jesus is very clear. He laid it out in his first sermon in his hometown. He said, 'The Spirit of the Lord is upon me to preach good news to the poor, sight to be blind, liberty to captives . . .' So the good news is social, material and spiritual. It's the integration of all of those.

Often we who look at the Bible and life through a Greek lens say the spirit and the soul is eternal. That is what gets saved and goes on. The body and history and all those things that are physical; that just decays and goes away. That's actually not a Christian view, and it might surprise your listeners to hear me say that. That's actually a heresy known as Manichaeism.

The Christian view is the resurrection of the body. It's the body of Jesus with nail prints in his hands and spear marks in his side. It says resurrection doesn't obliterate the pain and historical struggle. What you did which was eternal in life and the body is resurrected. It says, 'As you did it to the least of these, my brethren, you did to me'—fed, clothed, visited in prison. In other words, these social acts, these acts of earthly mercy, are eternal. They are as eternal as preaching the gospel and seeing someone confess their faith and saying their soul has been saved.

The good news is what Jesus said: it is good news for the poor. And I have to say, too often in our churches we hear preachers, unlike the great preachers of old, preaching prosperity for believers not justice for the poor. We cannot follow God and turn our hearts and eyes away from those who are poor. So the good news is integrated: social, political, economic and certainly spiritual.

What do you think are the greatest issues of justice and mercy for us today?
Without doubt the greatest moral issue of justice is why 30,000 children will die by the end of the day from not having enough food, from dirty water, from not having access to the medicines you and I take for granted. Most of those kids will be below the age of five. This is the great scandal that cries out to the Lord, because these are loved by him, made by him, and carry his image. They are those whom Jesus died for.

September 11 was terrible. Three thousand people innocently died. But that day 30,000 kids also died and it wasn't reported. And it happened the next day, and the next. So that is why World Vision exists; that's why a number of other Christian humanitarian organisations exist. To say in a world where we have solved the problem of supply: How many mobile phones does a teenage girl need to choose from? How many digital wide-screen TVs does a family home need? We have solved the problem of supply, and yet 30,000 children still die.

From that there are a number of major justice issues that have to do with allowing people to live peacefully and within their borders without their own governments preying on them. I'm thinking of Sudan, I'm thinking of Zimbabwe. Having governments act justly, not corruptly. The fastest thing that ruins a nation is bad government.

Then you cascade down to a range of issues that are much more local. What does it mean for Australians to be reconciled with the Indigenous? How do we deal with Third World conditions and find a way of dignity and responsibility for the Indigenous? That is our shadow and the scar on our soul.

Those are the sorts of issues that I think are the big ones.

Any of those issues could take a whole lifetime's worth of energy to work on. How do you even begin to select and focus your life on one?

I say to people pick three issues. Pick one that is *global*. It might be HIV/AIDS or how we beat malaria (and we could do that easily if we just had the will), or a particular country like East Timor given its proximity to us. Become informed about that issue. Study it, make it a matter of prayer, and maybe visit it.

Then pick a *national* issue. That might be Indigenous needs, or boat people, or asylum seekers. It might be a range of issues that you decide to be informed of and even write letters about.

Then thirdly pick a *local* issue. It might be youth homelessness in your municipality, the need to plant trees and do the green thing, or a school program that needs mentors. Here at World Vision we have a wonderful program called Kids Hope where Christians are invited to mentor, mainly in primary schools, just one student— usually a troubled student who teachers desperately need help with. It is a wonderful program having huge success.

So an international issue, a national issue and a local issue. Make them yours, make them personal and get connected around them.

Philip Yancey

GOD SEEMS RATHER DOUBT-TOLERANT, ACTUALLY

Where Is God When It Hurts? What's So Amazing About Grace? Disappointment with God. The Jesus I Never Knew. Rumours of Another World. Prayer: Does It Make Any Difference? Philip Yancey sits in his den tapping out books that inspire millions. On one September night in 2007, Philip dropped by Open House for a chat. An intriguing discussion ensued about God, doubt, family and the musings of an author with more questions than he has answers.

The last time we spoke I ended the interview by asking what the next book would be about, and you said that for the first time in your life you didn't know. Have you had any ideas since?

I think I'm going to do a memoir. I've done these heavily researched essay-subject-type books for the last twenty-five or thirty years, and I've covered those big questions that were floating around in my mind. Not that I've answered them, but at least I've explored them. I want to do something different. I have talked about my own background here and there in my books, but there are many stories I haven't told. And there are some challenges that I still face because I am going to be telling the truth, talking about actual people, some of whom are still living—and they know lawyers! I don't know exactly what I will be getting into. But I think I want to try that.

Any working title yet?
Not really. I'm simply trying to remember what has happened in my life so far and add some perspective. It's probably going to be about a three year project.

How about something original like, oh, 'Where is God When Yancey Finds Amazing Grace?'
I had a funny experience once. Some friends came skiing with us in Colorado. These folks happened to bring a Polish nanny to take care of their kids, and she expressed interest in my occupation. 'Have you ever written a book that was translated into Polish?' she asked. I replied that I thought so, and went over to my shelf of foreign books and looked for one that had a lot of 'c', 'z', 'w' and 'x' type letters in it—you know, a lot of consonants. 'What about this one,' I said. 'Is this one Polish?' 'Yes, yes,' she said, and got very excited. 'Well, what does it say?' I asked. 'It says, *Disappointment with Mould.*' I shot her a puzzled look: 'Are you sure that's what it says?' 'Oh no, no,' she corrected herself. 'You see, the words for mould and for God are similar. It actually says *Disappointment with God.*'

So I went back and retitled my books. Early on I wrote a book on the history of penicillin, called *Where Is Mould When It Hurts.* The bacteria develop resistance so I wrote a sequel called *Disappointment with Mould.* I teamed up with a doctor and wrote a book called *Fearfully and Wonderfully Mould.* Later I updated the work with *The Mould I Never Knew* and *What's So Amazing About Mould?*, and not long ago wrote a guide to cleaning refrigerators called *Finding Mould in Unexpected Places.*

[Laughter]

Where Is God When It Hurts? has probably been the biggest-selling book you've written. You were twenty-seven or something when you wrote it, weren't you?

I was, and I had no right to tackle the problem of pain—this daunting problem that philosophers and others have grappled with over the centuries. On the other hand, I had to. I write books because I can't stop thinking about something. I need to find a way through the thicket, the jungle.

I was working as a journalist at the time and I did a series of articles for *Reader's Digest* magazine called 'Drama in Real Life'—all these blood and guts stories of being attacked by a grizzly bear in our country or a crocodile in your country or stuck in a blizzard. And as I interviewed people I asked these (primarily Christian) interviewees how the church responded. Very often they would say the church actually made things worse. They'd be lying in a hospital bed trying to recover, trying to rebuild strength, and Christians would come in with a variety of pat answers: 'You must have done something wrong, so God is punishing you'. Or, 'No, it's not God, it's Satan'. Or, 'Well, it's not really Satan, it's God, but he has chosen you especially to demonstrate this or that.' I would hear these stories and I wouldn't know what to say. So when I don't know what to say I write a book about it, and writing the book gives me the chance to spend a long time interviewing, gleaning from others, reflecting, looking at the Bible and just trying to find my way through the issue.

Where Is God When It Hurts? is thirty years old now. Looking back, would you describe yourself as an old soul in a young body?

Good question. About ten years ago I had the assignment of going back and revising the book. It is an interesting process to revisit something twenty years removed in time, believe me. I could remember writing it, could remember each sentence, but my style had changed. I went through and added a lot of new material, but I tried to retain the basic structure and the basic material. That was quite instructive. I guess when I went over it I felt like I was a young soul in an old body when I first wrote it, because I kept thinking what right did I have to come up with that twenty years ago.

There is a kind of brashness to age and, frankly, when I am around young people they keep me fresh because they voice the questions that we wish would go away. A lot of young people will try to pin me down on something: What kind of car would Jesus drive? Nobody can figure that out, but it's a good question. They will pin you down on an issue that the rest of us old folks just want to ignore.

Were you always an inquisitive child?
I was, though I attended a church that had no room for inquisitiveness. If you doubted, if you questioned, you sinned. I learned to conform; you really had to conform in a church like that. But at the same time those deep doubts, those deep questions, didn't really get answered in a satisfactory way. The dangers of a church like that—and there are still churches like that, even in Australia—is that by saying 'Don't doubt, just believe', you don't really solve the doubts. They tend to resurface.

Later I found that God seems to have a lot more tolerance for doubts and questions than we do. The Bible is full of flawed people, people who doubt. When I go to college campuses, for example, I'll challenge the philosophy students to find a single argument against God from people like Bertrand Russell or Voltaire—and now it would be Richard Dawkins, Christopher Hitchens and people like that—that isn't already voiced in the Bible. Read Job; read Jeremiah, Habakkuk, Psalms.

'You have the freedom,' I tell them, 'to reject God, to disbelieve in God.' We are given that freedom. Indeed, we were given the freedom to crucify the Son of God. I personally respect a God who not only allows us to doubt, but gives us the material we can use to doubt him. God seems rather doubt-tolerant, actually.

I've learned that inquisitiveness and questioning are inevitable parts of the life of faith. If there was *certainty* there would be no room for *faith*. I encourage people not to doubt alone, to find some people who are safe to doubt with, and to doubt their doubts as much as their faith. But don't try to deny it and don't feel guilty about it, because a lot of people have been down that path before.

I know from your story that your dad passed away when you were about one year of age. Members of your childhood church suggested he come off life support, believing that God would heal him.
Right. This was during the days of the great polio epidemic when polio was every bit as feared as a disease like AIDS is now. We didn't know where it came from. Swimming pools were closed, sometimes schools were closed and in one year alone 50,000 people in the US died, as I recall.

My father was twenty-four years old, a young man, planning to be a missionary in Africa, and he came down with polio and was placed in an iron lung. A group of Christians gathered around him and could not imagine that it would be God's will for a prospective missionary to die at that age. So together, and with his complicity, he was removed from the iron lung. Ironically, he had a remarkable recovery for a few days. He actually went from total paralysis to having some movement restored. But then within a couple of weeks he died.

I don't know about the others, but my mother was scarred by

that experience for life. And perhaps that may partly explain why the first book I wrote was on the problem of pain.

I learned through the experience that what you believe makes a huge difference. Theology makes a difference. In this case well-meaning Christians believed that they knew God's will, and they were wrong. So it's important to know what you believe and to have those beliefs straight.

How do you think not having a father throughout those essential childhood and teenage years affected you and your understanding of God?
As I told you, I will be writing a memoir so I'll be trying to figure that one out!

Give us a sneak peek now.
Like any child, when you grow up you think this is normal; you can't imagine any other life. So I couldn't imagine having a father. Men were scary to me. My mother would use them as threats: 'I'm going to get so and so to come over here and blister your behind!'

God did a very great thing for me after I was an adult: he gave me a substitute father, a gentleman who has affected my faith more than anybody else. His name was Dr Paul Brand. We ended up writing three books together. He was truly a great man, and I was privileged to have that time with him at a time when my own faith was up in the air in a lot of ways. I was distrustful, I had been burned by the church and here was a person . . . it's as if God smiled and said, 'Philip, you have seen the worst of what the church has to offer. I am going to show you the best. Here is Paul Brand. Follow him around, analyse him, write up his life story.' And Paul stood up to scrutiny.

It only takes one person like that who is really transformed by God to make you think there must be something there. I got to know Paul as well as you can get to know a person. That was my job for ten years: following him around. And he changed my life.

Beautiful story. Let's take some calls. Brian is in Canberra:
Philip, I'm a writer myself. What you do when you get writer's block and you just can't create?
That would be every day! I started off as a magazine editor and I learned never to sit around and wait for inspiration. I just go to my desk and keep plugging away. Once I get something down on paper I can always go back and find a way to make it a little better or at least find out what's wrong with it. But when I'm sitting there with a blank page or a blank computer screen and there is nothing on it, boy, that's when I hit the wall that you describe.

I've learned to do what I call a 'guilt-free' draft. I force myself to keep typing, even though it sounds like drivel, and even though I am getting all these voices in my head saying *this is terrible, this is such a cliché, you've already said this, this is boring*, I force myself to keep going. Before I do that draft I spend a lot of time in preparation. Sometimes my outlines are as long as the chapters I write. I just keep putting words down. And the next day, when I take a look at it again, it's almost never as bad as I originally thought.

Jonathon is in Greensborough. What's your question for Philip?
You talk about this a bit in What's So Amazing About Grace?, but I'm wondering how Christians can love gay people.
I've learned that it really doesn't take grace to love someone who is like me, someone who agrees with me, who sees the world the same way I do. The real testing point for grace, where the rubber

meets the road, is when we are around people who are different than we are. And to me that is one of the great distinctives and great challenges of Christianity. Jesus said, 'Love your enemies and pray for those who persecute you.'

I've talked in my books about my friendship with Mel White. He was my friend long before I knew he had a secret life, and eventually he came out openly as a gay person and as a gay activist. When people say, 'How can you be friends with somebody like Mel?' I say, 'Well, how can Mel be friends with somebody like me?' I'm a sinner too. I'm full of pride, temptation and greed. And it's easy to rank sins. It's easy to say this sin is a lot worse than that sin. The Bible doesn't seem to do that. Whenever it mentions sexual sins, it also mentions things like pride, envy, even disobedience to parents. We all fail in different ways.

I know a man who would say he is an ex-gay person. He got married, feels his orientation really changed, but he still has a lot of compassion and sympathy for gay people and he runs an AIDS ministry. He said to me once, 'What I've learned is that Christians get very angry at other Christians who sin differently than they do.' It's not so much a question of whether we sin or not. We do. Some sin differently, and I try to put myself in their place and see myself through their eyes rather than vice-versa.

Vivian is in Sydney:
I was talking to a guy that was involved in the artillery in Vietnam. I was trying to tell him the gospel, and he said, 'It's hard to be a Christian when you have seen what I have seen.' With all the wars in Iraq and things like that, is God really kind?
It's funny how God gets blamed for a lot of things that actually

we humans are doing to each other. You know, we spoil the earth and have unjust economic systems and then we ask God, 'Why are there poor people? Why didn't you give us more resources?'

If you look at history, a lot of the wars are for the worst of motives—just plain greed, and power grabbing. And to turn that as a question to God—'How can you possibly allow this?'—man, how easy it is to blame God for things.

Many of those questions I have of God, God tends to throw back to me. Questions like, Why are there poor people? Why is there war? God throws these back to me. What are *you* doing about it? I think we as Christians should wrestle with those issues. The Iraq war is certainly one, the environment is another, justice, poverty in Africa; to me those are God's questions to us, and I'm glad to hear that you are wrestling with them.

Philip, in many of your books you'll mention your wife Janet. And you speak very favourably of her too . . .
Well she screens all those books. I can't get anything bad about her in there!

She is very different to you, isn't she? You are more or less an introvert and she is quite an extrovert.
She is indeed.

She's a social worker, and she's been involved in hospice work.
Right. In Chicago she headed up a senior citizens' program run out of our church, working with real down-and-out folks. Then when we moved to Colorado she became involved as a hospice chaplain. Now she works in an assisted living nursing home complex.

What does Janet bring to your life and writing that readers don't realise?
I wrote an article one time called 'They also serve who only sit and click'. That is a line I adapted from John Milton. I talked about the difference in our days. When I wrote the article she was a social worker in Chicago and she would come home with incredible stories, like the family she discovered living in a car under a bridge for six days who hadn't had anything to eat. She brought them in and fed them. At the dinner table she'd tell me such amazing stories almost *every day*. She is colourful and entertaining and I'm just captivated. Sometimes those stories appear in my books. They're good material.

And then she would look at me and say, 'And what happened in your day?' I would have a moment of panic and try to think. Then I'd say, 'Oh yeah. At two o'clock I found a very good *adverb*.' And that was the most exciting thing to happen all day! It's the difference between the kind of work she is doing—which is out there with people—and the kind of work that I'm doing—which is alone.

I've never heard you mention anything about children in your books.
That's because we don't have children. It would be hard to imagine life with children. I can barely get through a day as it is. We have a very busy travel schedule.

We have a rich, full life. I'm not sure who is going to visit us in the nursing home one day. We have lost, I'm sure, a lot of the joy and rediscovery of life that children bring. But we've gained too. We have gained by trying to use that time in other ways.

I've talked to many people over the years who will have one thing that they wish was different. They might say, 'I wish I was married', or 'I wish I had children', or 'I wish I *didn't* have children.'

I don't find a lot of help in dwelling on things that can't change. We seem fascinated by cause—why did this happen? The Bible doesn't really give us a lot of help on the issue of cause. In fact, it tends to switch the focus to our response: Now that it has happened, what are you going to do about it?

There are people listening, I know, who have things about your own lives that you don't like. And if you want you can fixate on those things and spend a lot of time trying to get answers from God on why they happened. You may find answers and you may not. I know a lot of people who never do. The Bible generally does not give an answer to the 'why' question, but what it does say is that no matter what has happened God can turn it into a good thing in your life and can redeem that grief, even that painful thing, into something good.

Andy is in Glen Waverly. What's your question for Philip?
When you finish a book, do you ever get those voices of doubt in your head that it isn't worthy? I'm a budding writer myself and when I finish a piece of work, I guess I doubt whether someone should read it. Do you ever experience that?
Oh, every time I write. What helps me is that I have developed over the years a group of friends that I really trust. There are maybe four of them. Frankly, I have a hard time finding friends who will truly be honest. Most of the time when you give a manuscript to a friend they want to be nice to you. They make you feel good, but they don't help your writing.

So you need to find a friend who is totally honest, who will tell you, 'I am so bored, I am falling asleep all over your manuscript'! When you write a book a couple of hundred pages long you know there are some good sentences, some good words, some good thoughts in that book, and then there are other things that should not end up in the next draft. So I've learned to get some trustworthy readers who will help me filter them out. It is very hard for you to do on your own.

Philip, out of all of your books, which one has most changed you?
I thought you were going to ask which was my favourite. I always go back to *Soul Survivor* because it was so fun to write about the people who have changed me. But in terms of the book that actually changed my behaviour it would probably be this most recent book on prayer. I really did learn a whole new way to pray, a whole new conception of what prayer is supposed to be. I was a very poor pray-er going into the book. I didn't value it, I didn't practise it very well, I felt guilty and inferior. But when I emerged from the book I felt the process had changed my whole attitude and practice of prayer.

Bring all the pages of Prayer: Does It Make Any Difference? *down to one great lesson for you personally. What is it?*
When I was writing the book, I used the phrase 'keeping company with God' as a working title. Prayer had been this little thing that I did, the spiritual discipline I would do each day. I began to see it more as a spiritual *privilege* rather than a spiritual discipline—keeping company with God throughout my whole day, in all the details of my life, not just that little time I'd have with him in the morning.

In Soul Survivor *you went into a fair bit of detail about the kind of churches you were involved in as a teenager and how in many ways they turned you off the faith for a while. At least one of those churches was incredibly racist, wasn't it?*

130

It was. I don't know if your listeners know about this, but there are Christians over the years who have believed in the 'curse of Ham'. They would say that dark-skinned races were actually cursed by God. I can remember my pastor standing up and saying that part of that curse is that dark-skinned people will always serve light-skinned people. They make good waiters and waitresses, cleaning your hotel rooms and things like that, but they can never really hold any kind of management position or be leaders.

Well, one day during high school I won some award and as a result I got to be an intern at the Centre for Disease Control. It was a very sophisticated laboratory. When there is influenza, a new strain or something like that, CDC is the place where top scientists analyse it and figure out what to do. I knew that my supervisor was a PhD in biochemistry and highly respected. I went in and opened his door and he turned out to be an African American. And I had one of those light bulb moments: my church had lied to me. It began a major crisis of thinking because I started wondering if they were wrong about other things too.

It's dangerous when the church takes a false stance on an issue. The South African church has formally repented of apartheid. It was their theological doctrine and now they have declared it a heresy. That is a very healthy thing. We need to be really sure that our pronouncements are biblical, and of course, what my church was teaching was not biblical. The danger is it's easy for a person who feels betrayed to reject everything else the church teaches.

These days do you ever have an inner reaction to African American people or to people with coloured skin, because of that early indoctrination?
I feel shame, because I know that reaction used to define me as a child growing up. I used to tell jokes and mock people of other

races. I would have to say there is a lot of our African American culture that is not my preference. I have no appreciation for rap music, or that kind of strutting athletic chest thumping. But that is a cultural thing, and certainly not all African Americans are like that. I've just learned, look, let's stop seeing people as a member of a race and look at them as individual human beings. There are some things about this person that I like and some things that I don't like, but I'm commanded to love. I'm commanded to fan the flame of the image of God in each person I encounter.

After all you've been through, the toxic churches, losing your father, after all the ups and downs and questions and doubts, why are you still a Christian?

I will have to be honest with you, Sheridan, and say one reason is that I haven't found a better alternative. And I've looked, I really have. There was a period of time when I desperately wanted not to be a Christian because it's not an easy thing. I have to care about things that I would rather not care about, subject myself to things that I'd rather be selfish and greedy about. Jesus doesn't let you do that.

But I would also say that as a journalist the people I have been around who I'm most attracted to, whom I have learned from, those people I most want to emulate, are people who in their own individual ways have become followers of Jesus. So I backed into the Kingdom, as it were, kicking and screaming, to borrow a phrase from C.S. Lewis. And part of that was because when I did my job, at the end of the day it was the people who were changed by God and whose lives were transformed and touched by God whom I wanted to be like. And I wanted to know the God who had nourished that life in them.

Alister McGrath

Alister McGrath is one of the world's leading Christian thinkers, with professorships held at Oxford, Cambridge and King's College, London. He studied mathematics, physics, chemistry and molecular biophysics before turning to theology and his special interest of the relationship between faith and science. Formerly an atheist, McGrath has written over thirty-five books on Christian belief, including *Dawkins' God, The Science of God, The Twilight of Atheism, The Order of Things, Christianity's Dangerous Idea, The Open Secret* and *The Dawkins Delusion?*

Talking to Alister McGrath is always an enlightening experience and choosing which discussion to include in this book was difficult. The following is drawn from two interviews in which McGrath recounts his move from atheism to Christianity, and gives his response to Richard Dawkins' popular book *The God Delusion.*

I read somewhere that atheism initially excited and inspired you. I never thought that atheism could excite or inspire anybody. How did it do that for you?
Well, it certainly did that for me back in the 1960s when I was at high school. Atheism seemed to promise a brave new world. The world around us was tired and worn out, and atheism talked

about a new vision for humanity. There would be no God and no religion, so this source of conflict would be removed. Like many people at that time, I saw atheism as a profoundly exciting but also a profoundly realistic vision. We didn't just think it was great, we thought it was right as well.

When you talk about God and religion being a 'source of conflict', are you talking about the various conflicts between countries?
I grew up in Northern Ireland. Northern Ireland has many attractions I'm sure, but one of the downsides is that it has these endemic religious tensions. I was growing up in Belfast; I saw this all around me. In fact, I was at high school when what we euphemistically called 'the troubles' began in a big way. That reinforced my view that religion simply led to violence. It was a very simple message but one that I found very credible at that time, and certainly that was something that played a big role in sustaining and developing my thought as an atheist back then.

That would be what many still believe today—that religion is the world's greatest evil. How would you respond to somebody who says that now?
Well, I think there is no doubt that religion does cause violence. So does atheism. So does animal rights. So does politics. You think of the enormous amount of political violence we've seen in the twentieth century. You think of the dreadful human rights records of the Soviet bloc and the mass exterminations that were carried out under Stalin and so on. The real issue here is not actually religion, or indeed anti-religion. It is something about *us* that means that sometimes we are inspired to do some very good things and sometimes we end up doing some very, very bad things.

I think a realistic account of human nature says the big issue here is extremism of any kind. That is the common enemy. One of the reasons that I think religion is so often singled out in this respect is that so many people are religious, so it's very easy to establish a correlation between religion and violence. But actually the truth is much more uncomfortable: it is something about *human nature* which ultimately drives people to use violence for those things they regard as being of supreme importance.

So you're initially inspired and excited by atheism. When did the vision begin to fade for you?
It began to fade just before I came up to Oxford to study chemistry. I was very, very excited to be studying science at Oxford. I was absolutely sure that it would reinforce my atheist faith. In fact, as I reflect on the way I felt about things then, I was a bit like Richard Dawkins is today. But unlike Dawkins I was very interested in the history and philosophy of science. As I began to look into that, I began to realise that things were rather more complicated than I had thought. In fact, the quest for secure, reliable knowledge was much more complex than some of the simplistic messages I'd received from atheist writers.

There were two things that really made me begin to change my mind. One was a growing intellectual scepticism about the intellectual credibility of atheism itself. The other was beginning to realise that Christianity had a lot more going for it than I'd thought. As I went up to Oxford, met Christians, and actually read Christian writings instead of accepting second-hand, often rather distorted accounts of these, I began to realise here was something that was not simply intellectually exciting, but actually had the potential to change people's lives. And I think that was really the tipping point for me making my way to becoming a Christian.

I would like to explore both of those points in a little bit more detail. You say that you were starting to doubt the philosophical underpinnings of atheism. Tell me more about that.

I had been brought up to believe simplistic nostrums like 'science disproves God'; incredibly simple things like that. When you're a young person simple things are easy to believe. And I think one of the things you have got to cope with as you get older is that life is actually a lot more complex than that. And certainly as I began to look at some of these simplistic slogans, they simply did not hold water. In fact, all of my big concerns about people like Richard Dawkins is that they keep repeating these things, even though Dawkins is now in his sixties. That does puzzle me a bit.

But I think the real issue is this, if I can put it very, very simply: I cannot prove to your listeners that God exists with absolute certainty. But neither can an atheist prove to your listeners with absolute certainty that there is *no* God. And therefore, the Christian and the atheist take their positions as a matter of faith. Given that we can't prove either, the big question is: What other factors are there that might incline us towards one position or the other? It is at this point that I think the huge explanatory capacity of Christianity, its ability to make sense of the world and help us get bearings as we ask what the purpose of life is—Where are we going? What are we here for? And how do we make sense of what we see around us?—that it all comes home to present an extremely attractive, but also extremely credible, vision of the world.

Was there one thing in the Christian faith that caught you?
I think at that stage the thing that excited me most was its capacity to change people's lives. But Christianity is a strange thing, isn't it? You begin by being attracted to one aspect and then as you grow into it you discover that there are all these other aspects as well. I have now discovered other things that I didn't know about when I was younger, and these have given me added excitement and given a new sense of direction to me subsequently. It's a bit like exploring a new country; there is so much territory to discover.

Alister, why did atheism start to capture the Western imagination in the first place?
Atheism really became significant in Western culture in the late eighteenth century and then very significant in the nineteenth. I think there are a number of factors here. One was, if I can put it very simply, that Christianity—particularly state churches—in western Europe were seen to be oppressive, and atheism offered liberation. You can see that in the French Revolution, which in its early years had a significant atheistic agenda. Also, it began to make a very powerful appeal to the imagination. People were so used to a Christian way of thinking about the world that a radical new alternative was quite exciting. So it was a liberator and it promised a brave new world as opposed to the rather over-familiar world that was given by Christianity at that time.

In The Twilight of Atheism *you say that philosophical arguments against God have turned out to be circular and self-referential. Can you give us a simple example of that?*
A very good example would be the kind of arguments you find from Ludwig Feuerbach, Karl Marx or Sigmund Freud. Basically

they would argue, look, there is no God, but people believe in God so we have to offer some explanation why. Now, Feuerbach locates this in the way we develop the idea of an object, Marx in social pressures and Freud in psychological pressures. Then they all say there is a perfectly natural explanation for your believing in God which, of course, confirms that there is no God.

But the real problem is that they have actually presupposed the conclusion: the whole argument being *there is no God, and therefore we need to offer an explanation of why people believe in God.* They begin from their conclusion. The obvious alternative is to say, well, the reason people believe in God might well be because there *is* a God. And, of course, they have to exclude that possibility as a matter of principle; and therefore the whole thing becomes a little bit circular and self-referential.

I guess you wouldn't expect that they would offer it is a possibility.
Actually, some atheists are extremely honest and will say, look, we can't be sure about this but at the moment we feel that the best way of explaining the world is to say that there isn't a God, but we're keeping our minds open. I can respect that, I certainly can.

Richard Dawkins' book The God Delusion *spent months on the New York Times bestseller list. What do you put the popularity of the book down to?*
I've asked many people who have read the book why they find it so exciting. It's very interesting. Christians who read this book say, 'This is just awful as a representation of what Christianity is.' Those who dislike religion, and there are a lot of us around, find it gives intellectual legitimation to their position. In other words, they don't believe in God and they see this book as saying, 'You're right,

and this gives you intellectual respectability.' I think that really is the key to this—it's about intellectually empowering people who already have very gut-level reactions against believing in God.

You respond to Dawkins' book in your The Dawkins Delusion? *Let's explore some of the ideas raised. Dawkins says that he would change his mind the moment somebody presented evidence of a God to him, but nobody can. What are Dawkins' criteria for proving the existence of God? What kind of evidence is he looking for?*
That is a very good question, and one of the difficulties I have is he is asking for evidence that really can't be provided for *any* belief system, including atheism. Nor democracy. Nor, in fact, anything that really matters in life. This is one of the big problems you find in relation to *The God Delusion*. Dawkins says in effect, you have got to be able to show this to be absolutely, one hundred per cent right or with a tiny, tiny, margin of error. How many things are there in life that you can be absolutely that sure about?

The point I try to make in responding to Dawkins is that, first of all, atheism itself is a belief system. Really, if you want absolute certainty on this, the best position is agnosticism—saying we can't be absolutely sure, so therefore we decide not to reach a decision at all.

The big realisation for me has been that for an awful lot of people there is this belief that unless you can scientifically demonstrate something it can't be believed in. Of course, there is a very big question here about the limits of science, and Dawkins is very, very silent on that.

What are the limits of science, then, in this discussion?
Well, let's take a very prominent scientist—Sir Peter Medawar,

who won a Nobel Laureate prize for medicine back in the 1960s. In his book *The Limits of Science*, published twenty years ago, he says that when it comes to understanding how nature works, how the material order hangs together, science basically has no limits at all. But when it comes to questions of meaning or questions of value, it can't answer these. Not just that it can't—it can *not*. That is an extremely important point. Dawkins seems to have this idea that science in some way is able to answer all the big questions of life. Certainly there are many who would like to believe that, but I simply want to say that is not so.

At what points then can science bolster faith or provide some sort of apologetic or explanation that there could be a Creator?
Well, there are many things we could say. One is the remarkable order in the world. Why is that so? More than that, why do we as human beings have the capacity to actually make sense of it? That points to there being some inbuilt ordering and design to the way the world is, and something very significant is our capacity to realise that. Of course, if you are a Christian, this gives you a very important point to make here: both the world and we are created by God; there is a resonance in the way the world is and the way in which we think.

While Richard Dawkins says he wants to eradicate all religion, it seems to me he's primarily attacking the Christian God. You've debated Dawkins. Does he actually have a good understanding of the Bible?
There is a section in *The God Delusion* that is about the Bible, and I have to say it really is very, very weak. It seems to me to rest upon visiting a couple of atheist websites and singling out quotes which are taken completely out of context and very often not simply understood at all.

He has this very weak discussion of Jesus. He argues that Jesus, in effect, created this 'in group'/'out group' mentality that was just about reinforcing traditional Jewish values. I find this astonishing. I mean, even Richard Dawkins will have heard of the parable of the Good Samaritan, which is about breaking *down* those kinds of barriers.

Dawkins is highly selective about the Old Testament passages he deals with. He simply cherry picks bits of the Bible and Christian tradition that suit his purposes and completely ignores those which speak otherwise. For example, the whole Old Testament prophetic emphasis on the need for social justice, the need for personal integrity, the need for mercy in our dealings with others—those aren't talked about at all. So I would have to say it is a very skewed and biased representation of the Bible there.

Anyone can take the Bible and read it as they choose, but Dawkins does not really ask how Christians read the Bible. He interprets certain passages in ways that I as a Christian would find bizarre. For example, he interprets certain Old Testament passages to mean that Christians should, if they are being consistent, execute their children for disobeying them. Now you and I both know that no Christian would dream of doing that. Dawkins presents this as if this is the way things actually are.

Dawkins has said in the past that the story of Joshua in the Old Testament is morally indistinguishable from Hitler's invasion of Poland or Saddam Hussein's massacre of the Kurds. How do you respond when the war scenes of the Old Testament are raised as a sign that we have an evil God?
Well, that is a very significant issue and certainly for any Christian the conquest narratives are really quite difficult to deal with. I think

what we have to say is, that may well have been a very distinctive period in Israel's history, which in no way legitimates that being applied to additional episodes in, for example, Christian history or indeed in our own day and age.

I think Dawkins makes a very important point there that this kind of war and massacre is outrageous. Let us also bear in mind that some dreadful things happened during the Soviet Union, when, for example, this kind of oppression was used against Christians by atheists. One of the most astonishing things in *The God Delusion* is Dawkins' assertion that atheists would never dream of using violence against anybody else. There is a bigger problem than either religion or anti-religion here; there is something about human nature which makes it very, very easy for us to lapse into violence.

Dawkins also says that belief is an accident of geography—if you are born in the West you're likely to be a Christian; if you're born in an Islamic country you'll be a Muslim. Does he have a point? Is it all simply geography?
Well, there is no doubt that the circumstances of your birth affect not simply your nationality but the dominant belief system you have. But Christianity is a missionary faith, and one of the reasons why is because it believes it is applicable to all people. Christianity is not a national religion like Hinduism or the classical religions of Greece or Rome. It says, 'This is for all people at all times and makes sense everywhere.' Christianity sees itself as building on what is there in other cultures, but at the same time bringing them to fulfilment. In Christ we see the partial truth of other faiths being brought to their absolute fulfilment.

Dawkins himself would argue that we need to believe in science, and where science isn't found in the world then you need to take it to bring light to people. In many ways Dawkins and I would adopt a very similar approach; it's just that we differ about what we are bringing to people.

Dawkins has quite a bit of missionary zeal himself. In the book he says, 'If this book does as I intend, religious readers who open it will be atheists when they put it down.'
He's an evangelist, isn't he? He is very clear that he wants to convert people, and he describes those who believe in God as 'dyed in the wool faith heads'—which doesn't strike me as a very promising start for a dialogue. I think there is a real issue here: Dawkins is angry. One of the questions I ask myself is, why? I think the answer partly is this: on the basis of his analysis, religion ought to have died out ages ago. I mean, none of the arguments he puts forward in this book are actually new. In fact, I tried to date many of the arguments he uses, and I think the date 1890 is quite a good one to apply to them.

I think what Dawkins is saying is, God ought to have been abandoned years ago; he hasn't [been] so let's give him the final shove. And yet, for people who read this book, by the end of the four hundred pages, they feel that he hasn't made his case. Certainly those who are already atheists like what he is saying, but those who are religious believers and those who are in the middle find it a deeply disturbing book, because it's so aggressive and dismissive.

Do you have any idea why Dawkins is so angry?
Well, I did ask him this once. I can understand that Dawkins doesn't believe in God. But most of my atheist friends in Oxford are atheists who are very quiet about their position, and certainly are extremely respectful of those who take different perspectives.

I have to say to you that I know of nothing that adequately explains the anger. It really puzzles me. It's as if religion is like a red rag to a bull here. It's not a rational thing; it's something deeper, it's emotional. But I cannot find anything that adequately explains it.

In the book Dawkins has a rant about the God of the Old Testament, calling him 'arguably the most unpleasant character in all fiction. Jealous and proud of it, a petty, unjust, unforgiving control freak, a vindictive bloodthirsty ethnic cleanser, a misogynistic, homophobic, racist, infanticidal, genocidal, filicidal, pestilential, megalomaniacal, sadomasochistic, capriciously malevolent bully.'

I'd want to say this in response: Dawkins clearly doesn't believe in a God like this, and neither do I. The reason I don't—and this is an extremely important point—is because I read the Old Testament through the light of the life, death, resurrection and teaching of Jesus Christ. For Christians, Jesus is the lens through which we read the Old Testament. He is the fulfilment of the Law and the Prophets and therefore we read them through his example. When you do that you see God in a very different way.

What Dawkins is rejecting is a very patriarchal Jewish idea of God, which the New Testament utterly transforms. This is why I place so much emphasis on the importance of Jesus Christ. Dawkins seems to think that Jesus rejects the Old Testament idea of God. He doesn't—he transforms it so we see God as he is meant to have been seen.

Dawkins says that we don't need religion to motivate us to be good. He says morality is a quality that has evolved in us—we've developed altruistic genes enabling us to have empathy. How do you respond to that idea?

I think the longing to be good is part of being human. The real issue is how do we *know* what is good, and if we long to do what is good then how are we *enabled* to do it?

Dawkins himself is very clear that science cannot tell us what is right and what is wrong. Therefore the basic longing to do what is right needs to be informed. What are the standards that we're trying to aim for?

Iris Murdoch was a very well-known atheist writer some years ago here in Britain. She made the point that unless there is some concept of good that is beyond us, and above us, which we cannot change, which we have to try and grasp, then really we might as well just be doing what each day and age thinks is right. The question of what actually is right seems to rest on there being something beyond, something transcendent, which we try to imitate and respond to.

I'd agree with Dawkins in that we all want to do what is right. The real issue is how do we decide what is right. Stalin thought he was doing what was right in trying to eliminate religion and bringing about his atheist agenda.

Dawkins also believes that raising a child as a Christian, a Muslim or in any faith is basically child abuse. How do you respond to that kind of statement?
Well, I see he is making an important point. He is saying that you cannot ram belief systems down children's throats; they must have some ability to respond to them, evaluate them critically.

There are two things I would say in response. Number one, I think *The God Delusion* makes the case for the necessity of good religious education. My real concern would be what might happen if, for example, atheist parents decided to ram *The God Delusion* down their children's throats and said, 'This is what Christianity is like.'

But more than that, Dawkins seems to be advocating a system of educating children which actually excoriates religion, which involves getting religion out of things all together. I think that is both unrealistic and simply unjust. There is a real need, which is enshrined in international law, for people to have the right to bring up their children in their own religious tradition, irrespective of what the children may subsequently decide. So I am very worried this is Big Brother atheism trying to impose its views on family life.

Alister, if you could say one thing to the many who've read The God Delusion, *what would it be?*
I would simply say, look, this is a very unfair book. What we really need to do is ask why so many people believe in God if the case is as bad as Richard Dawkins makes out. The answer might just be that the book is thoroughly unfair and misrepresents what God is all about.

Tony Campolo

Dr Anthony Campolo is many things: a speaker, author, sociologist, university professor, pastor, social activist and passionate follower of Jesus Christ. Tony has pioneered programs for the poor, counselled US Presidents, and over his many years of speaking, writing and lecturing, challenged millions around the world to live radical lives of Christian service.

As book titles like *20 Hot Potatoes Christians Are Afraid to Touch*, *Speaking My Mind*, and *Following Jesus Without Embarrassing God* suggest, Tony Campolo tells it how he sees it, and is not without controversy. In one of our many conversations, we talked about Tony's life, message and mission, and those who have influenced him the most.

You're seventy-two now, right?
I won't be seventy-two until February, but yeah, I'm getting up there. My idea of a happy hour now is a nap!

You're doing more than many thirty-year-olds can do. How many years do you think you've got left at this pace?
I have no idea. I seem to have the same energy that I had years ago, so I don't see myself slowing down until I begin to feel it. I don't feel it yet.

Have there ever been moments in your life when you weren't in control of everything that was on your plate? You seem to cope with things so confidently.

Well, I head up a missionary organisation that I founded some years ago called the Evangelical Association for the Promotion of Education. We have some 300 workers working in three Third World countries, as well as in nine cities across the United States. There is so much that goes on with the organisation and for a long time I was trying to run it all in addition to everything else I was doing. There were times when things were coming at me from twenty different directions and I didn't think I could handle it all. I finally had to go through a process of reorganising the work, giving away portions of the work to certain people who work under my and the Board's direction. So I don't feel the stress I once did.

But there was a time when I was pretty stressed out simply trying to do all this stuff in places where there was need among poor and desperate people. Oh my, I had so many problems. Every day there was something somewhere in the world that had been messed up, and I was constantly stressed trying to figure out what to do. I don't know ninety per cent of what goes on in our ministries these days because other people are running them and they only talk to me when they feel they have to. So life has gotten a lot simpler and all I have to do is speak and write and teach.

You've travelled the world but from what I know you still live in the city of your birth.
That's right.

You're still a member of your childhood church.
You've got it.

Tony Campolo

And you're a professor at the same university you graduated from.
That's right. I've been teaching there for thirty-seven years.

Is there something to that—being planted somewhere?
Yes there is, and it goes deeper than simply wanting to stay in the same location. I think that if you are going to live a consistent Christian life you have to be connected with a community that knows you and that can hold you accountable for how you live. There are four of us who live in this immediate neighbourhood where I live and we have committed ourselves to staying close to each other, looking after each other, ministering to one another. We meet whenever we can, and that is usually once a week, when I'm able to be there. We pray with each other, check up on each other, we're involved in each other's lives.

I think that in a society like ours, where people tend to live highly individualistic lives, people get into trouble. I think that's what happened to Bill Clinton. I think that's what happened to Jim Bakker and Jimmy Swaggart. They lived individualistic lives and there was no accountability group: people who had known them all their years, who weren't impressed with them because they knew them 'back when'; people who could ask the serious questions that needed to be asked if these men were to be kept on track.

Living in a situation where people know you and can hold you accountable for what is going on in your life, who can see deviations from the standard life that Christ has called you to live—everybody needs a group like that. That's why I have stayed in one place. These are the people who can hold me accountable, and I need that just as they need that.

149

If you were to reduce your life's work to one sentence, what would it be?
'He challenged young men and women to minister to the poor holistically; preaching the good news of Christ and ministering to the needs of the poor, socially and economically.'

That's not bad for something I just threw on you. You've been living it so many years though.
You know, when I was forty, my friends and I—the same people I was just talking about, we're all the same age—we all took two days off by ourselves. We said to ourselves, we're forty years old and if we live to be eighty that will be wonderful. We're at the halfway mark. What do we hope to achieve in the next forty years?

We talked and then we eventually wrote our responses down. What I concluded that I needed to be doing the rest of my life was this: I wanted to so live and so give myself to other people that when I hung up my sneakers when life was over, there would be at least two hundred young men and women working among the poor in urban America and in Third World countries doing holistic ministry—bringing people to Christ, carrying on programs of education and cultural enrichment, carrying on programs that would enable the people they were serving to live the kinds of lives that God had called them to live.

That's what has kept me ticking all these years. We were very specific. We wanted to say, 'This is what we want to do and this is how many people we want to reach.'

Do you know what the figures are now?
Yeah, we're a little over 1400.

Well, isn't that wonderful! You've not just met the goal, but doubly exceeded it.

It's good, and we're still plugging along. I think it's important for every person to take a tablet of paper and a pencil and go off somewhere and ask a very simple question. Here it is: When my life is over and I'm lying in the casket, and they're having the funeral service and people are talking about me, what do I hope they are saying? Write those things down. Write down what you hope your family is saying, your friends are saying, the people at your church are saying, the people in your neighbourhood are saying, the people around the world are saying. Write those things down, then put them up on a wall and everyday ask yourself if you're becoming the kind of person that people will say these things about. Define your goals, define your purpose, know what it is that you want to become—not just what you want to do, but the kind of person you want to become.

Great exercise. You're well known as a speaker and a preacher. Who has influenced your speaking and preaching in the past?

Probably my mother more than anybody else! My mother was not a preacher but she was an incredible storyteller. We are Italian, so people would gather around in the evenings and on Sunday afternoons and mum would tell us stories. She would tell Bible stories and she would tell stories of life. She would excite people and describe things with such detail that you could picture them, you could imagine them, you could sense the situation she was describing. Her ability to communicate was absolutely wonderful. Her style, her manner, her way of delivery is something that I have imitated; it was from her that I learned how to communicate.

What about your social conscience? You've spoken on almost every issue imaginable, whether it's politics, the homosexuality debate or the Iraq war. Could you point to one particular person who helped nurture that?

Well, my father was a union organiser. Now that's different! Christians aren't very involved in labour unions. Generally if you look around, you find groups like the Christian Businessman's Association, The Full Gospel Christian Businessman's Association. Everything is businessman, businessman. My father was a member of a labour union and consequently he looked at social problems from the working man's point of view. As we sat around the table in the evening, my father would share his concerns about the poor people he knew, about the people who were getting their teeth kicked in by the establishment, about the people who didn't have hospital care, who didn't have a decent income, people who were marginal and were having a very difficult time surviving.

So I grew up with this mother telling me Bible stories and my father telling me about people who were in need. Then beyond it all I came to the most revolutionary book in the world, and that's the New Testament.

As I was growing up I would read these things in the New Testament. I wasn't hearing it in the church but I found it in the New Testament. The church didn't necessarily move in a pacifist direction, but Jesus certainly did when he said, 'Blessed are the peacemakers', 'Overcome evil with good', 'Those who live by the sword, die by the sword'. When I read the Bible I began to get these radical viewpoints. There are over two thousand verses of Scripture that call upon us to respond to the needs of the poor. That some of my Christian brothers and sisters didn't see the commitment to ministering to poor people and rescuing people from poverty with a Christian calling seemed strange to me since it was on every other page of the Bible. I wondered whether they were being moulded by politicians or by the teachings of Scripture.

I mean, the Jesus of Scripture is very, very different than even the Old Testament. In the Old Testament, for instance, you get the concept of tithing. But when you come to the New Testament, Jesus never asks us to tithe—he calls for total surrender. He says to the rich young ruler, 'You want to be my disciple? Go sell whatsoever you have and give it to the poor, take up your cross and follow me.' If we were into tithing in the New Testament, we would have to rewrite the hymn book. We would have to sing *'One-tenth* to Jesus I surrender.' Can't you just hear the chorus? 'I surrender *one-tenth*! I surrender *one-tenth*!' There is no question that the Jesus of Scripture calls us to a level of commitment that is radical indeed. So if I seem to be radical it's only because in a small way I'm trying to approximate the teachings of Jesus and those teachings come forth in the New Testament.

That has come through so strongly in your life and work. Have you ever said something that you've later regretted?
Oh yes. If you're at the cutting edge and if you're really speaking as forthrightly as I do, there are some things that you're going to say that will be downright wrong. I can't say that I think exactly the same way now as I did ten or twenty years ago. I think that the Christian life is one where you grow in insight, grow in perspective, grow in the way that you look at things.

As I've gone through the years and as my critics have pounced on me, I've listened. I think you learn a great deal from those who criticise you. Whenever I receive letters of criticism, the first thing I do is spend a little time in prayer asking God if this person is saying something that I need to hear. Rather than going on the defence, to listen seriously to see whether there is validity to the criticism that is given.

Now, I get a lot of criticism that I'm glad about. There are some things that I say which people get upset by but I don't care because after careful reflection from Scripture I think what I said is in accord with the teachings of Jesus. Jesus says, 'Blessed are ye when they persecute you'—when they revile you, say all manner of evil against you—and the next phrase is important: 'for righteousness' sake'. If after careful reflection I conclude that what I said is in line with what Jesus is teaching, at that point I write back to the critic and say, 'I'm sorry you feel this way about me, but I'm not sorry I said what I said because I think it's in accord with Scripture.'

This continually comes back to what you believe about the Bible. How did your passion and trust in the Bible come about?
When I was a high school kid, in West Philadelphia in the United States, there was this accountant who lived in the neighbourhood. He wasn't a theologian; he was an accountant. On Saturday nights he would get the young people in our neighbourhood together and do a Bible study, going through books of the Bible verse by verse, chapter by chapter. In my high school years I think we went through Luke, Philippians and Ephesians. We went through the Bible Saturday after Saturday night, an hour-and-a-half at a time. Out of this group came nine ministers, fourteen missionaries and a couple of professors of theological seminaries. This ordinary layman who had never been to Bible college, all he did was study the Scriptures as best he knew how, loved us and he ministered to us and, above all else, he taught us to love the Scriptures and to see them as an infallible source for faith and practice in our everyday lives.

You are no stranger to controversy. Do a website search on 'Tony Campolo' and for every site saying you're a saint there's another saying you're a heretic. It's probably because of some of the controversial issues you speak on. Do you think at times you've been misunderstood?
Well, there are people who don't like some of the things I say and they can't get back at me about them because they're obviously true.

A case in point: I contend that if you're going to be a follower of Jesus then it's all right to make lots and lots of money—but it's not all right to keep it. If you're going to follow Jesus you've got to live sacrificially. You have to use all the resources that God has placed in your hands, insofar as it is possible, to take care of your own family at a simple lifestyle, but then to minister to others. So I get into trouble when I say that I don't see how a person can be a Christian, a follower of Jesus, and own a BMW.

Just imagine Jesus was living in Brisbane, he needed to get a car and he had $80,000. He could buy a second-hand car from Hertz for $12,000—a perfectly usable car that would last the next fifteen years if he takes care of it—and he could use the other $68,000 to feed the hungry in the world. Or he could take that $80,000 and go out and buy a BMW. Which do you think Jesus would do if he was in the world today? When you make that type of statement, every BMW owner in the world gets mad at you. Problem: my critic can't get back at me because he knows I'm saying the right thing. He can't imagine Jesus going out and spending $80,000 on a BMW when there's a world of suffering and need out there.

Church ministers get mad at me because I say if God had a choice between buying a new stained-glass window, putting in a new organ and putting new carpet in the church, or feeding the hungry people in Africa and addressing the AIDS crisis with the money, I know which he'd do. Ministers get mad at me, but they're not going to argue with me on that point. Instead they wait for me to say something that they can take out of context and use in such a way as to make me look bad. But what they're really doing is trying to get me back on things that I said where they were vulnerable.

A teaching of yours that's proven controversial is your belief that Jesus is present in every human being. Not just the Christians, but every human being. Some feel that's walking close to New Age or pantheistic thinking. What about the fact that it's only Christians who have the Holy Spirit living within them?
Let me be quite frank. Let's go to the Bible. Remember I said earlier that the Bible is my guide for faith and practice? Look at John 1:12, and that whole first chapter of John. 'In the beginning was the word. The word was with God, the word was God.' It's talking about Jesus there. 'The word became flesh and dwelt among us and we beheld his glory.' Then listen to verse 9: 'and he is the light that lighteth every man that cometh into the world.' How many men? *Every* man that cometh into the world. That's not my theology; it's the theology of John.

I believe that you can resist the Spirit of God. But if you become a Christian don't think on judgment day you're going to be able to take the credit. It was his Spirit motivating you to believe in him. It's not you—you wouldn't believe in him, because without his presence there would be nothing good in you whatsoever. You can resist the Spirit, you can say no to the Spirit; but please understand that if you become a Christian it's because the Spirit of God motivated you to go towards Christ. So he is alive in every human being.

I always quote Matthew 25 where Jesus talks about feeding the hungry and clothing the naked: 'Inasmuch as ye do it unto the least of these my brothers and sisters, you do it unto me.' Jesus says whenever you see a needy person, whether that person is a Christian or a non-Christian—if you are looking at some needy person in Africa suffering from AIDS or if you're looking into the eyes of some sick person on the streets—if you're filled with the Holy Spirit you will have this eerie sensation that Jesus is staring back at you. Jesus chooses to present himself to you through that person.

Now, why pick on me? Pick on John, pick on Jesus, but don't pick on me. I haven't got an idea about God being a mystical Spirit waiting in every human being to be loved from any other place but the Scripture.

Now, that doesn't mean that that person is a Christian. A person isn't a Christian because the Spirit of God is in him. A person becomes a Christian when they surrender to the Spirit of God and say, 'Jesus Christ, you can be . . .'—now, here's a word that we hate to use, because we think we just have to become 'believers'. Not so. No, you have to say, 'Jesus Christ, you can be *Lord* of my life. From henceforth, I will be what you want me to be, I will do what you want me to do, I will go where you want me to go. I am totally surrendered to you.' It's in surrendering your life to Jesus that you become a Christian.

We have reduced Christianity into believing certain propositional statements and if you say these statements are true then you're a Christian. Oh no, it's not simply a head trip. It's the surrendering of your life. It's the giving over of all that you are and all that you have to Jesus Christ, saying, 'Here I am, Lord, invade me, take me, change me, use me—I am at your disposal, you are the Lord of my life.'

Tony, if there was one character trait of God that has become most precious to you in recent days, what would it be?
Well, the obvious answer should be the love of God. It's the dominant motif of God. 'God is love.' That's in First John.

But second to the love of God is the joy of God. If you go to the list of the fruit of the Spirit in the fifth chapter of Galatians, it says the fruit of Spirit is first of all love, then secondly, joy. When I think of God, I am thrilled with the fact that this is a God who doesn't come with sombre expression, but comes to lighten our hearts, to lift us out of the miry clay, to put a smile on our face and joy in our hearts. 'I have come,' Jesus said, 'that you might have joy and that my joy might be in you and that your joy might be full.'

Lord Chesterton once said that God is the only child left in the universe because all the rest of us have lost our childlike sense of joy because of sin. I have a grandson. I throw him in the air, bounce him off my knee, put him on the floor, and he yells, 'Do it again, pop, do it again!' By the fiftieth time he is hysterical with joy. I often ask my students, 'How do you think God created daisies? Do you think he just created one daisy or a billion daisies at once?' I think he created one daisy and something inside of the majestic heart of the great God of the universe said, 'That was fun, let's do it again.' He created daisy number two and he said, 'Do it again.' Then daisy number three and four, and fifty billion trillion daises later the great God of the universe is jumping up and down and clapping his hands saying, 'Do it again, do it again!'

I believe in a joyful God and I believe that when you surrender your life to him, you not only experience his love, you experience his joy.

He's a *fun* God.

Michael Frost

Over the past decade a new Christian movement has surfaced in a
variety of Western nations: a body of Christians wanting to reshape
how church life is done and how the Christian life is lived in a post-
Christian, post-modern culture. The umbrella term for this collection
of thinkers and missionaries is the 'emerging church', and while the
movement is broad, its essence is to rediscover something of the vital,
organic nature of the Christian church's earliest days.

Michael Frost is an author and Professor of Mission at Sydney's
Morling College. He is considered one of the leading voices of this
growing phenomenon.

Your latest book is called Exiles: Living Missionally in a Post-Christian
Culture. *Let's unpack a few of those phrases. What do you mean by
'post-Christian culture'?*
The book basically assumes that we in the West live in a world that
was once anchored or rooted in basic Christian principles or beliefs.
They formed, if you like, the bedrock or foundational values that
created the culture of which we are part. So in many respects you
might say that our nation Australia is a 'Christian nation'. But now
at the beginning of the twenty-first century we must come to our

senses and recognise that if Australia was a Christian nation, it is no longer. It may still have a whiff or resonance of some basic Christian assumptions, but in truth we are living in a highly secular, post-Christian—meaning post-church—society. Once it was conventional and proper to belong to a church—whether Catholic, Protestant, Anglican or Baptist—but now those aspects of Australian culture have almost completely disappeared.

About ten per cent of the Australian population would say they attend church, but in terms of very committed, devoted followers of Jesus who are focused on reading the Bible and living as Jesus asked us to, it could be as low as two or three per cent. So how might we follow Jesus in a world where people aren't interested in church attendance by and large?

How about 'missional living'?
Most people would be familiar with the term 'missionary'. You think of someone who might go overseas to serve the poor or to build churches in an unchurched culture. Well, I want to appropriate that kind of language and make it a bit more hip and a bit more useful in a post-Christian world. If we acknowledge that Australia is post-Christian and post-church, is it not reasonable to assume that engaging as Christians in Australia today is not that different to being a missionary to New Guinea in the 1950s or to Africa in the 1850s, in the sense that you are representing a faith and a lifestyle that your culture might not necessarily endorse, encourage or even appreciate?

If we are going to represent Jesus in such a world we need to think of ourselves as missionaries. I don't mean with pith helmets, running off to the cannibals or what have you, but in the sense of moving out into the culture of which we are part—serving the poor, living well, being good friends; having more of a 'go to your world' mentality rather than an expectation that it will come to you.

And 'exiles'?
Well, almost smack bang in the middle of the Old Testament we have a thing called 'the exile', where the Babylonian army of Nebuchadnezzar conquers Israel and drags all the Jews back to Babylon as slaves. They become exiles in a foreign culture.

A good swathe of the Old Testament actually is written out of the experience of the Jews at that time. They are trying to be faithful to following the God of Israel, but they have to do it in a world which doesn't accept, promote or encourage that faith. Numbers of theologians and biblical scholars have begun saying, gee, maybe there's something in that Old Testament material that is useful for people today wanting to be faithful followers of Jesus in a world that is not Christian.

Has the traditional church lost some of the essential message and mission of Jesus?
Oh, I think so. I think that the church, and I am talking very generally here, is still operating on an assumption that our nation thinks that church is good. If we just got it right they would come. And there are some churches that are obviously getting it 'right'. Some churches are booming with lots of people who enjoy attending; they are dynamic kinds of places. But they are very few and far between.

To think missionally is a call to say, look, some churches are going to appeal to people for whom church-going is still attractive. But what are we going to do about the ninety per cent of the population who couldn't give a toss?

In the book you talk about new forms of church that can look very different from the traditional steepled building we typically think of. You describe a group that meets on Sunday mornings to go skiing and a mothers' group that actually has a lot of the elements of a church in its activities. Are such groups really churches, though? When is a church a church?

Well, that's the $64 question. Ask anyone on the street what 'church' means and I guess, by and large, they're going to say, just as you've said, a building with stained-glass windows and steeples. Even if they're thinking of a big contemporary church like Hillsong, they're still thinking of a building and programs, events and services.

If you think seriously about what the Bible thought church was when the word was first coined, there was no such thing as church buildings. The church was an underground movement of Jews and Gentiles who had come to put their trust in Jesus. They had no buildings, no clergy, no seminaries, no programs, no money, and in some cases, certainly in Rome, they were actually persecuted. So what did *they* think the word meant? What they thought it meant was a collective of people who had oriented their lives around the person and teaching of Jesus; who had been set free by his teachings, his life, his death and his resurrection; and who had made a commitment to fostering a devotion to building each other up in that faith and reaching out to those around them, whether they be the poor or those in need of hearing this message of Jesus.

When you think about church in those terms, it makes sense of the radical church growth that you see in China, for example, which from 1949 to 1989—just forty years—grew from two million people to about eighty or ninety million people, possibly even one hundred million people. How did they do that with no buildings, no property, no programs, nothing? The first Christians in the first century had none of the stuff we think church is, and probably the most dynamic movement of the church in the world today has none of it either.

Telling, isn't it?
Yes, it is, because you will find the same thing happening in Vietnam, in some places of Northern Africa and South America. Whenever the church has blossomed, it has usually done so without the benefit of all the stuff we normally assume a church needs.

What about church discipline? Can a group that gets together on a Sunday morning to go skiing exercise discipline if one of its members needs to be gently nudged back into the fold, so to speak?
Yeah, sure. But don't underestimate how many Christians sitting in the pews of conventional churches every Sunday aren't getting disciplined. The assumption is always that the conventional church will do church discipline better than what seems to be more organic or chaotic new modes. But I have been in lots of churches where some of the most despicable behaviour is going on unchallenged and undisciplined, even though it has all the bells and whistles of a 'proper' church, so to speak.

Look, the guys who do the water skiing up in Brisbane don't just meet to water ski. They meet to serve the whole water skiing community on the Pine River. They bring extra spare parts and if anyone else's boat breaks down they stop what they're doing and go and serve them. They actually run a gathering on picnic tables around by the river where they pray, they take up a collection, they give money away to the poor, they break bread, they drink wine, they do the sort of stuff that Christians are called to do when they gather. But the other feature of what they do is they actually serve a particular community. On that river the same people come back every weekend to water ski and picnic. There is a real sense of community there, and these guys are actually known by some of those people as the chaplains of the Pine River.

What are some of the more exciting, radical or fresh initiatives of church that you've seen flowering around the world?
Basically, they are groups of people who have identified a particular 'people group' to serve. I know a bunch of guys up in the northern suburbs of Perth who have identified new home buyers and they move into areas and help people lay their turf on the front garden, build a deck on the back of their house, and run street barbecues. They've identified a series of streets where new houses are going up and have sold their homes and bought in there in order to 'incarnate'—that is, embody—the life and work of Jesus amongst suburban new home buyers.

I know a bunch in Adelaide who are all into amateur theatre. They've joined various amateur theatre groups and likewise are meeting together, breaking bread, praying, studying the Bible, serving the poor, giving money away and building relationships within the amateur theatre fraternity.

I know people who have started alternative churches, for want of a better word, in tattoo parlours in Pittsburgh, and in shoe stores in San Francisco.

A church in a tattoo parlour!
You should see these guys! There are two couples and a single bloke. They started their own parlour in Pittsburgh, called 'In the Blood Tattoo and Piercing Parlour'. When I met them, all their arms and as much of their body was covered in tattoos. They just opened this

as a business, and the next thing you know they had Goths, outcasts and other kinds of marginalised people in their neighbourhood just hanging out in the store. They had nowhere else to go. So they said, 'Well, on Monday nights, why don't we read the Bible together and break bread?' And they have led all these people to Jesus, and three or four churches have spun out of this tattoo parlour.

So in a sense the missional movement is this: anybody who recognises what it is to be a follower of Jesus and who has a sense of affinity with a people group, go to them, take people with you and fashion community right there in their midst.

A key word you use there is community, and it's something you talk a lot about. True community, if we can use such a phrase, is much more than simply meeting together on a Sunday. You use a sociological term, 'communitas', that describes a quality of community or friendship that emerges when groups of people are thrown into some sort of crisis together. You think the church should experience that kind of community?

Well, I think that's exactly the quality of Christian community that you find all the way through the pages of the New Testament. If church for you is just a meeting that you attend on Sunday you will never know it.

As you say, *communitas* is just the Latin term for community, but it's used to identify something different from that kind of warm, fuzzy, mother's milk-type, 'we don't fight with each other' community where you have a cup of tea after church and everyone talks about the weather. It's polite and it's warm, but if you call that community sociologists say, hang on, there has to be something that is richer and deeper than that. So they ended up going back to the Latin word *communitas*: a group of people who are bound together by a common cause.

Most of your listeners will have been on a sporting team, or if they're involved in the church they might've been on a mission trip somewhere. They'll know what it's like to have felt this really delicious sense of intimacy with a group of people all committed to a common cause, each pulling their weight, but doing something different; collectively being greater than the sum of the individual parts.

Any ANZAC Day you see all those old diggers sitting around for a beer together. That's because they had *communitas* and fifty years later it is still rich and real for them. So I say if we are in a post-Christian world, that creates perfect conditions for us to move out and serve the poor, to preach Jesus, to love others, to build relationships, recognising that none of us can build on our own. We need each other.

Group dynamics will limit the degree to which people can have that kind of community with each other. Will the emerging church movement only ever be a small church movement?

If I go back to the church in China, it's now one hundred million people strong and made up of churches of no more than a dozen to fifteen people. In fact, it is illegal to congregate in a group any larger than fifteen people. So the church in China—thanks to the communist regime—has to (a) meet in homes, because it can't meet in public buildings, (b) meet in groups of no more than fifteen people, and (c) can't train leaders in seminaries. Put those three categories together and you've got a recipe for something quite remarkable. Because when they grow to twenty people it's like, yikes, we'll get into trouble so you ten better go off to so-and-so's home. This cellular division thing is what has produced this phenomenal church growth.

I don't think the church has to be limited to fifteen. But it is hard to imagine having that kind of intimacy with five hundred or a thousand or twenty thousand people. But it's been proven that you can have a church of one hundred million people doing this in groups of fifteen or twenty. If I had my way, that's what I would love to see in this country. I would love to see a viral movement unleashed, where we haven't all got to have the buildings and the right bits and pieces for us to be church, but we can actually be launching hundreds, thousands, of alternative, emerging, missional or whatever term you want to use, communities of people who are followers of Jesus, serving others and doing everything that the Bible says they should do but don't look anything like what you might conventionally think a church should be.

You've got your own church experiment happening called Small Boat Big Sea. *How would you describe the group?*
We meet in Manly and most of us live around there. We are a group of people who have made a commitment to do a bunch of things with each other and within the neighbourhood of which we are part. That is, to bless each other, to eat together regularly, to listen to God's voice, to learn from each other and to recognise that we are all sent into the world as missionaries. Whether you are a stay-at-home mum, or a lawyer, or a film maker, photographer or in my case a theological lecturer, you are sent into that world. The values that we are committed to kind of make up the acrostic BELLS: to bless, eat, listen, learn and be sent.

You would be amazed at what happens when a bunch of people just make the commitment to do those five things. I don't commend those as *the* way to do it; there are lots of ways to do it. But if you are a bunch of people committed to blessing each other and blessing your community, I can tell you here and now it will win you lots of points in your community. There are lots of churches whose neighbourhoods are none the wiser about what they do behind those doors every Sunday and wouldn't have a clue that the church has any interest in them at all.

So how do you bless other people?
You can bless them by performing acts of service, by speaking words of strength into their life, by giving gifts; there are all sorts of ways. We really want Manly to be the best neighbourhood it can possibly be, and we think that we can make a contribution to that.

Eating is important too, because we happen to think that eating is a really significant way for making connections with other people. Eating is not just refuelling so that you can go on and do other stuff. Eating is actually 'the stuff' and you would be amazed by how many references in the New Testament there is to eating: to Jesus eating, to Jesus' friends eating, to the early church eating. In fact, the central kind of religious rite of the Christians was breaking bread and drinking wine. So eating with each other and eating with people that don't yet know Jesus builds enormously rich relationships too.

In Exiles *you include the story of Spanish painter Bartholomew Esteban Morello. I think it might be a good story to end on.*
Well, Bartholomew Morello was a young Spanish boy raised in Seville in a fairly libertine kind of family. Both his parents passed away, he was the youngest of a lot of kids and all his brothers and sisters had left home. So effectively he was orphaned and handed over to his aunt and uncle who were actually a very austere, religiously controlling family. He chaffed under this shift from his family of origin to his aunt and uncle.

One of the symbols, I guess, of the fundamentalist regime that he was struggling against was a painting that they had in their lounge room. It was of Jesus the shepherd boy wearing a perfectly clean white smock, perfect Roman sandals, rosy cheeks, clear blue eyes, a halo—your standard kind of stained-glass window Jesus.

Morello would look at this picture regularly and think, 'What kind of boy is that? I mean, he doesn't even seem like a boy; he seems like a ghost or a phantom.' So one day when his adoptive parents were out, he took the picture down off the wall, pulled out his paint set and thought he would do a bit of touch up on the picture. He turns Jesus' halo into a big straw hat; he grubbies up Jesus' cheeks; he turns the piercing, frightening eyes into mischievous eyes; he rips and tears up Jesus' smock; he puts scabs on his knees; he turns the lolling lamb at his feet into a young puppy dog, and the perfectly straight shepherds crook he turns into a gnarled walking stick. Morello then has a picture of Jesus the shepherd boy who looks just like a boy he could hang out and play with.

His adoptive folks come home. As you can imagine, this wasn't just vandalism for them; it was sacrilege. So they belted him within an inch of his life and made him carry the picture down the street of Seville to let everyone know what a terrible burden they had. Morello was then noticed by another painter, taken on as a protégé, and the rest is history. He became the most famous painter of his time.

I love the story because I think in many respects it is symbolic of what I find myself doing an awful lot in my life. I feel like I run into people's houses and pull their pictures of Jesus off the wall and I vandalise them. I feel like I just want to open people's eyes to the Jesus in the Bible—you know, the Jesus who was not well behaved, conventional and middle class, but a man who actually agitated conventional people so much that they wanted to kill him, and indeed did kill him. A man who ate with all the wrong people, misbehaved regularly, whom religious leaders found to be completely radical and unacceptable, a man who I think in lots of respects probably wouldn't even qualify for membership in lots of our churches. A man who I think should remain the troubler of the church's soul.

Jesus should be the comforter of the church's soul; Jesus should be the saviour and the lover and the redeemer. All of that I believe to be true. But we also need to let him be the troubler of our souls. Because when we become too conventional, too safe, too stuffy; when we become too out of vogue with the very people that Jesus loved to hang out with, we need him to remind us that we have gone astray.

When you look at the people that Jesus hung out with, we all know that they were prostitutes, tax collectors and those euphemistically referred to as 'sinners'. But the thing about them was that they actually *liked* hanging out with Jesus. Now you tell me, who are the people who hate the church more than anybody today? Prostitutes, and the equivalent of tax collectors and sinners. They despise the followers of Jesus. But in Jesus' time they loved hanging out with him. What does that say about how far we have got this wrong?

John Smith

John Smith is the founder and Executive Director of Concern Australia, the Superintendent of St Martin's Community Church in inner city Melbourne, and the founding President of the God's Squad Christian Motorcycle Club. Since its founding thirty-five years ago, God's Squad has become a respected part of the 'outlaw' bike scene. Its members have become travelling chaplains, responding to bikers' personal needs and even performing traditional functions like marriages, baptisms and funerals. John's autobiography, *On the Side of the Angels*, recounts the movement's growth throughout the world.

John Smith has addressed the United Nations, nearly faced execution in the Philippines and spent much of his life with outlaws and the marginalised, but in his early years was anything but the radical. Read on to discover how the once buttoned-up youth became a leather-clad preacher of peace.

You were a fairly conservative lad in your early preaching days, weren't you?
I was off the wall, mate. As a young guy I once went to preach in Mt Isa where I met a group called the Cross Country Singers. They sang lyrics like 'On the wings of a snow white dove' and back then even that sounded worldly to me! I grew up in a situation where

171

cards, pool tables, motorcycles and dancing were all considered evil and part of an ill-spent youth. At one stage I was so pro the Vietnam war that I actually said America should drop limited atomic bombs on North Vietnam and turn it into a landing field for B52 bombers so they could resist the creeping peril of yellow communism in East Asia. I held a white South African view of race, believing that the blacks were cursed of God and to be the subservient race to the whites—all that sort of stuff.

It was an incredible thing that within ten years I was an activist for equality without throwing in the Christian faith.

Coming out of such a conservative background, I went through a dramatic change. It was that revolutionary period at the end of the 1960s and early 1970s. I was a late starter in a sense—I discovered the Beatles the year they split up—but really got into it after that. My wife and I felt called to attend the Sunbury Pop Festival. It ended up costing me my job as a nice young preacher. I got sacked because the church thought there would be nudity and dope smoking, and that wasn't a suitable place for a young preacher to be. I thought that was the very place a young preacher should be to learn what's going on in the world, to be able to engage in conversation about it, and to have a compassion for a generation that really felt lost and uncertain about the past and the future.

We trotted off to Sunbury. It was bigger for Australia than Woodstock was for America in terms of the percentage of the population attending. One of the things I wrote in my autobiography was my reaction to Billy Thorpe singing 'Somewhere Over the Rainbow'. He had gotten the whole crowd shouting obscenities. These days you hardly see a movie where the magic words aren't found, but in those days that was pretty over the top. Billy was screaming obscenities, and all of a sudden in the midst of this angry high-volume music, he suddenly went into this almost mystical singing of 'Somewhere Over the Rainbow'. There were people all around with tears running down their faces. It was like a psychic wave of longing that went across that huge crowd from a generation that was longing to find something better.

After Sunbury we came home and found that the church had given us twenty-four hours notice and three months pay. I came home from the church office and Glena and I just stood around the sink and cried. Then we prayed. Some people who don't understand the religious thing are going to think the next bit is kooky, but it's true.

I had started a Jesus newspaper that grew to about 35,000 copies circulation each month. It was a twelve or sixteen-page tabloid that was first called *Truth* and later, *Truth and Liberation*. We'd just started putting that out and were getting phone calls and letters from young people that were sick of the system, both in and out of the church. We were standing around the sink, wondering how we were going to pay our mortgage, how we were going to survive with three little children, and how we were going to pay for the next edition of the paper. Glena said, 'You just need to go ahead with printing it and trust God.' I said, 'Where are we going to get the money from?' She said, 'Just send it off to the printers and we will trust.'

When I got back she was all smiles. A letter had come in the mail. 'I've been scared to open this envelope,' Glena said, 'because I don't know how much money is in it.' Inside was a cheque and a bunch of notes from a uni student in South Australia. And it was precisely the amount that it cost to republish the next edition of the magazine. I mean, this person didn't know that I'd been given the boot, and we didn't even know what the printing cost was going to be, but it was exact.

I know there are some who are cynical about Christians—and I think some Christians do carry on. But there are times when these kinds of events happen and there is no explanation that makes any sense, except that somehow God intervened in the real world.

That's the way we started. From then on we said, 'Well, Jesus was a friend of publicans, sinners and other outcasts; he hung out with the wrong crowd and that was probably one of the reasons he got crucified. So what will we do?' I started hanging around pool rooms and places like that.

I had seen some bikers on the side of the road, just drinking their beer and fixing up their bikes. And I said, 'Dear God, please do something for these guys.' And God said to me, as best as I understand it, 'Why don't you answer your own prayer?' Around the same time I met a guy who would've been England's equivalent to Evel Knievel. His name was Eddie Pye. He'd been a top stunt rider and had become a Christian. Eddie said, 'Smithy, you've got the ear of young people. Get out there on a motorcycle and that will help your cause.' So a whole bunch of events like that all came together and seemed to be saying, 'Go do it.' So we did.

Of course, God's Squad has been through its troubles. Bikers tend to be radically individualistic and a bit ego driven. It's been a struggle sometimes to make sure that people don't play an ego game with it. But now we're in Norway, Finland, the Ukraine, Holland, Germany, Ireland, England, Wales, all over Australia. One of our guys in Holland used to be a debt collector for the Mafia in Italy. His family broke up because his wife was terrified of what was going on. He was led to the Lord by some Christian bikers and today he's back with his wife and riding with our guys. It is really amazing where it has gone from those early days.

John, with all of these years riding with bikers, what one thing have you learned?
I would want to say that one size does not fit all. This week in the newspapers there's been another big thing about crime and the biker scene. I'm not saying that stuff doesn't happen. But there are some clubs that are just like *Rebel Without a Cause*, you know, the James Dean thing—blokes that say the system's stuffed, we don't want to have anything to do with it, we just want to be blokes on our bikes. There are others where individual members may be playing with drugs but the club overall wouldn't do that kind of stuff. Then there are some clubs that are pretty hardcore, involved in the international drug scene and so on.

But you cannot judge a book by its cover. That is one of the biggest things I've learned. And that's a Bible thing—both in the Old Testament, in Moses' writings, and also in the writings about Jesus in the gospels, it says, 'Man looks at the outward appearance, but God looks at the heart.' Working in this scene has led me to meet some of the most beautiful people who look like the wildest people you could ever see. Some of the guys who look the most outlaw love their kids, love their wives and are just the most true blue mates. In fact, honestly—and it's a terrible thing to say—but I have seen outlaws who are now sixty-plus years of age at funerals of their mates who frankly show a broken-heartedness and a connectedness to their mates that I rarely see even in church.

You're turning sixty-five this year. That's got to be reason enough to have a mid-life evaluation of sorts. What has been the most significant moment for you—the moment that has proved to be the unexpected turning point you never would have seen at the time?
Well, one of them comes before I started down this wild path. I had

some friends who were working with street kids in the inner city of Melbourne, many years ago in the 1960s. I went to see what they were doing. At that time I was at Bible college and I was dressed in a suit with a tie. I had no idea of that world and these guys introduced me to some of these gang kids. One of them looked at me and said, 'If you answer one question I might talk to you.' I was a Bible student and felt I would be able to give this kid on the street a good answer. He looked me straight in the eye and said, 'What is God like?' And without thinking what that kid's background was I said, 'God is like a father, son.' His eyes blazed with hate and he said, 'If he's anything like my so and so'—you can guess the words—'old man, you can shove him up your jumper.' Then he stormed off into the night.

I felt a little bit offended. I thought, I'm trying to be nice to this kid and he's walked away from me. The youth worker asked me what I'd said, and I told him I'd said that God was like a father. He said, 'That was real smart, Smithy. Do you know anything about that kid's father?' I said that of course I didn't. And he replied, 'Well, his father is a sexual abuser of his girls and his family, he's a drunkard, he beats him up and this kid is the only thing standing between this man and the death almost of his mother and his sisters. And you told him that God is like that.' Sometimes we come with our religious data and we do the tip truck thing and dump our theology on people. That was one of the most important moments for me.

A second important moment—and, you know, I get nervous sharing this because I don't want to sound like I'm some brave guy, because actually I'm a scaredy cat underneath—it was years ago while my wife and I were in the Philippines. We were at the World Congress on Evangelism, and this message came through saying if some of us delegates would come to Negros, we might be able to save a thousand people's lives. They had been warned over the radio that these death squad guys were coming in to wipe out nearly eight hundred refugees that had fled from the mountains when the government went in and dropped napalm on the farms to get rid of a handful of communists. They were about to come into this Catholic seminary and wipe everyone out. At about five o'clock in the morning my wife said to me, 'John, God has told me to go to Negros and stand between these people and death.' She was braver than me because where she was going looked very, very dangerous.

I then got a telegram from Mindanao. A mad mayor there, whose motto was 'Kill a communist for Jesus', had gone in and bulldozed down the homes of peasant people in a search for Japanese gold they assumed was left there in the last World War. We got invited by the people to go and monitor this human rights violation, and I felt that God wanted me there. So we wrapped up some little parcels for our children back in Australia, who were teenagers then. We wrapped them up and we hugged each other and cried . . .

[Sobs]

. . . we didn't expect that both of us would come back. We thought one of us would probably die. So we put these little parcel things together for the kids and wrote a letter to them in case one of us didn't come back

Then we set off—Glena to Negros and me to Mindanao. When I arrived there they had the bulldozers bulldozing down the homes. There were women and children running everywhere in terror, with these guys with M16 guns all over the place. My co-pastor and I just went ballistic—we jumped on one of the tractors and ripped all the wires out and stopped it. Then we got arrested and carted off to prison. They told us we would be executed the next day.

That night they interrogated us every hour or so. They would quote Bible verses and say, 'Jesus said, "You shall know the truth and the truth will set you free." Tell us the truth: who brought you in here? Then we will set you free.' That was a big test. There were about fifty people jammed into a cell the size of a small lounge room. Our only toilet facility was a can with part of the side cut out hanging from a string. We were laying head to toe on the floor to sleep. I'm lying there looking at these little white gecko lizards running across the roof thinking that I liked them more than human beings.

But that night I had to decide whether I really meant what I'd always preached. Because the temptation came—tell them a few names of the civil rights workers that brought you in; they're not going to know that you cheated on them; you might get free. My mate and I had to lay down that night and decide whether we really believed what we thought we believed—whether we really did believe there was a life to come, whether we really did believe that if we died there was a better life on the other side, whether we believed that it was better to die with dignity and commitment to truth than it was to save your life and live with what you knew was cowardice. We stuck to it and it looked like we were going to be executed. Some members of the UN came in and tried to talk to the mayor. They visited us and said, 'Look, there is nothing we can do. It looks like you are gone.'

And I must admit to having a certain incredible peace. It changed something in me. When I watch Christians conforming to the stock exchange, preaching prosperity doctrine and stuff, I feel sick now because I know what it is to face death and say: 'I'd rather have Jesus than silver or gold/I'd rather have him than riches untold/I'd rather have Jesus than anything this world affords today.' If you're not a Christian and you hear this you will think that I'm completely crazy, but it is something . . . you see it in Mother Teresa, you see it in much greater people than Glena and I—it is something that is so much bigger, so much more fantastically human, something so precious and great that goes beyond all this materialistic stuff.

Dear old Glena—she was on Negros and they had a conference with all these television cameras and everything because they actually stopped the massacre there. The death squads moved out of town and these mostly women and children were saved through the actions of Glena, another woman from New York and an Australian Uniting Church minister. One of the journalists said to Glena, 'Do you know that your husband is on the island of Mindanao and that he is awaiting execution?' And she replied, 'Praise the Lord!' They looked at her like she was a complete nut. Then she said, 'I don't mean that I'm glad that he's in danger. I just feel so good that he stood by what he believes. He has always preached this stuff to everybody and now he's living it.'

How were you freed then?
We got free really because of the international press. The journalists learned how the soldiers did their regular march; they would flit off into the shadows and then come out again when the soldiers were going around the other side. They pieced the story together, and we got out and left the next day. We waited until we had some escorts and then we fled the four-and-a-half hours or whatever to Davao. Even then, when we thought we were safe and went to a restaurant, our friends from the town recognised some the mayor's thugs coming into the restaurant, so we escaped out of four doors and ran off to a Catholic monastery, later got picked up and sent to the airport. It was a bit like being in a movie.

Absolutely amazing stories. Glena was overjoyed that you were living what you were preaching, and really that comes back to the person of Jesus. I'd like to end on this—what characteristic of Jesus most captivates you these days?

Ah, his unconditional and indiscriminative love. That is the most powerful thing.

Saint Paul said that *faith*, *hope* and *love* are the three things we need. I know so many people who have committed suicide. They were loved by their parents or by their friends, but they didn't feel any hope and so they still took their lives. So it's not only love that we need. We need a *faith* to live by—something that makes solid sense of life with all its pain and struggles. We need a *hope* in something bigger than ourselves. And above all else we need *love*, because Paul said you need those three, 'but the greatest of these is love'.

When I was a little kid we used to sing a song that said, 'Jesus loves me this I know, for the Bible tells me so.' I still feel like crying when I hear that little song, because the love of human beings isn't big enough. I saw people who came to Jesus at the end of the '60s and the beginning of the '70s because they were suicidal over the splitting up of the Beatles. A lot of the hippies that really loved the Beatles were devastated when these guys broke up, saying nasty things about each other, because they'd been the ones that said, 'Love, love, love—All you need is love', and it hadn't worked out.

I find something enduring and robust and different about the divine love that comes from Jesus. It's the greatest of all loves and it transforms your life—it transforms your attitude towards others and even towards things.

Don Piper

90 MINUTES IN HEAVEN

On January 18, 1989, Don Piper died. Driving back from a conference, a truck crossed his path and hit his car head-on. Paramedics arrived at the scene, found no pulse and covered Don and his mangled car with a tarpaulin.

But Don Piper was conscious—in heaven. Bright lights, pearly gates, winged angels . . . Don says he experienced them all before returning to earth and beginning the recovery process that continues to this day.

The instant you were hit by that truck you say that you weren't taken down a tunnel, carried towards light, or any of those things we typically associate with near death experiences. You say you were suddenly surrounded in light. What was your first thought after that?
Well, the first image I saw was the faces of the people who had gone before me. It was a head-on collision; I was driving at 50 mph, the truck was driving at about 60 mph, so the impact was about 110 mph. That's an incredibly brutal impact. So I had no reaction time and there was no sense of passing away, and I think that was why I was so instantly there. There was no ebbing of my life. It was just a split second impact until I was standing there.

And, you know, people often talk about near death experiences.

Ninety minutes is not nearly dead—I was very dead. I had four different sets of emergency medical technicians pronounce me that way. But I was oblivious about what was happening on earth. I was surrounded by all these familiar faces of people who had gone before me and, of course, they were breathtakingly beautiful. And it was a splendid reunion with these people who had told me about Jesus and invited me to church. Here I am immediately confronted with people who helped me get to heaven. So I knew exactly where I was because I knew where they were.

It didn't take very long for that realisation to occur?
No, I knew right away. I was looking at the face of my grandfather, and I had been with him when he died many years before, and actually rode in an ambulance with him to the hospital before they pronounced him dead. So the first person when I got to heaven was my grandfather. I was looking right into his face, and I knew right where I was. I was with him when he died; he was there to receive me when I died.

What did he look like?
He was recognisable as himself. In fact, I didn't see anybody that I didn't know. And I was very curious about that, as you might imagine, for a long time. Why did I only see people I knew? The only thing I can conclude is that the people who are sent to receive us at the gate are the people who helped us get to heaven, and that's the reunion that is part of the process.

They all looked perfect. In life some of them had been quite elderly—they had no teeth, or they lost all their hair—and yet they looked whole and complete in heaven. I must say, they didn't look complete in the sense that we are; in bodily form. It was a spiritual thing. The Bible says that at the end of time we'll have reconstituted bodies, perfect bodies and we will be reunited with our souls and they will dwell in the house of the Lord forever. But I did recognise all these people for who they were and they were quite breathtaking in their appearance. Almost glowing, but very recognisable.

And so I can't wait to go back. I really never wanted to come back. To know that they are there and they are waiting for me at the gate is something I earnestly long to return to.

Were there any children? Are there age differences in heaven?
No, I didn't see any children. And once again, the people who received me were the people who had a positive spiritual impact in my life. Even a couple of the people who had died before me in their teenage years were there, but they were not teenagers when I saw them. But I still knew who they were. People in heaven seemed to be ageless. So it's my conviction that the people who die as children or even babies, and in some cases unborn babies, will be fully constituted people. Adam and Eve were not created as children. They were created as what we would call adults, but created for fellowship with God. So I think everybody there is fully developed. I think that is the best way to say it. I didn't see any old folks either. They were just all people. Age is not an issue.

Tell me about what you saw. The depiction of heaven you write about in 90 Minutes in Heaven *almost sounds like a caricature of what we typically think heaven is like—pearly gates and white surroundings.*
Well, it's that, and as you might imagine, so much more. Even the people that try to describe heaven in the Bible, John and Paul and those folks that have endeavoured to try to describe heaven,

always apologise afterwards, because human earthly words cannot do justice to heaven in any way, shape or form. But the gates really were pearly or, I would say, pearlescent. They were glowing, they were glimmering, they were almost alive and translucent, but they really are pearly gates, a large magnificent edifice. And yet the entrance into the gates was quite small, almost big enough for just one person at a time.

I really did see golden streets. I really did hear the wings of angels all about me—just kind of hovering, ministering to all the folks that were gathered at the gates. I heard incredibly magnificent music that surpasses any that I have ever heard here on earth. All hallelujah songs, all praise songs, all glory to God songs, all holy, holy, holy songs being lifted up to the throne of God. And the remarkable thing is that there was no chaos. I could hear all this myriad of songs, thousands of songs, and I could distinguish each one of them with my heavenly ears. So heaven is a buffet for the senses. A sensory explosion. There are colours that don't exist here, sounds that don't exist here, even an aroma that is heavenly and . . . incomparable.

And what language were people speaking?
You know, it really wasn't a language I've ever heard before. We did communicate vocally, and yet there was communication that went beyond speaking. Here we are having an interview and that's the way we communicate on earth. We try to learn information, we exchange facts, we ask questions. In heaven there is never a need for questions. You really know when someone says something, the full scope and impact and depth of their statement, so you just exchange information back and forth. And it's perfect information,

fully understood information. The language was not comparable to anything that I have ever heard here. It's a heavenly language for lack of a better description.

So there is a sense of knowing, then.
Knowing—that's a perfect word for it. You know, the apostle Paul says that we see things now dimly as if through a mirror, but then we will see things as they really are. And in heaven you really do; you just know. Now, there is actual communication—people did tell me they loved me, that they were glad to see me. But I know I knew what they said, I knew how they felt about it, I fully understood the passion behind those statements.

Describe who else was at that welcoming committee for you, when you realised you were in heaven. Were any of your current day family members there who hadn't died at the time?
No. I only saw people who had died before me, people who had passed away. Obviously there were people remaining alive when this accident occurred who had also had a positive spiritual impact on me, but they had not departed yet, they were not there. So the group of people there at the gates were people who had had that kind of influence. They had told me about Christ. They had taken me to church. My parents were not regular church attenders in my younger days. So I was frequently taken by others to church. If I missed a Sunday these were people who called me on Monday and said, 'We missed you yesterday. Where were you?' There were teachers, aunts, uncles, relatives, a couple of classmates—it was a splendid, awesome reunion.

That is fascinating, because we often think that heaven is outside of time, and yet the people who met you there were people who in earthly time had passed away, not those who hadn't.

Indeed, it was almost if they had been waiting for me; and my conviction is, even though I have been back here now on earth for seventeen years, I think they are still waiting. See, I don't think any time has passed for them, because I didn't sense any passage of time in heaven. It's linear, it's propelled forward, and yet there is no sense of the passage of time. So even though the clock was ticking back here on earth and I'm in a wrecked car covered up with a tarp and an accident happened at 11.45 am and at 1.15 pm I'm returning because someone is praying over me—ninety minutes passed on earth—I didn't sense that I was in heaven for ninety minutes at all. It could've been nine hundred minutes or it could have been nine minutes. There are no clocks in heaven, there is no passing of time. And those folks are still waiting for me. They have just been joined by a lot of others that have gone since that time.

Did you see God?

No, I didn't. As I was approaching the gates and everyone turned to allow me to enter, I was entering in on these golden streets, and inside the gates are magnificent structures. You know, Jesus said in John 14: 'In my Father's house are many mansions. If it were not so I would have told you. I go to prepare a place for you.' So there are places prepared in there for the saints. As you go in it gets higher and higher, like an elevation, and even though it is utterly brilliant outside and brilliant at the gates, inside is even more intense, and the higher it goes up that crest the more brilliant it is. I know that's where Jesus was and that's where I was moving. When I got inside the threshold, suddenly my time there ended and I was back on earth under that tarp in the car with someone praying over me, and I was returned to earth.

Well, let's go to that moment. It was a church pastor who got out of his car, walked up to the accident, and felt an incredible sense that he ought to pray for you even though he'd been told that you were dead. Describe all that.

This accident happened on a very narrow bridge in the middle of a lake, so traffic was backed up for miles in both directions. This pastor—his name is Dick—was actually coming home from the same conference I had attended. We didn't know each other. He walked up onto the bridge and asked if he could be of any assistance. He was told that the man in the red car—me—was dead. God spoke to him. The moment the policeman said those words, God spoke to Dick and told him to pray for the man in the red car.

So, casting aside his theology, which had told him that there was no reason to pray for dead people, he went to the police and said, 'I have to pray for him'. The policeman said 'Sir, you obviously misunderstood. He's dead.' Dick responded, 'Well, I have to be obedient. God told me to pray for him.' So they argued for a while. The police finally relented and Dick got under the tarp and began to pray for me. He prayed for quite a long time.

By this time my church had been notified that I had been in a bad accident, but not that I was deceased. So they began a prayer chain that went all the way around the world; they are praying for me, not knowing I'm dead. Dick is praying, and singing hymns, praise, hymns—he alternates. At 1.15 in the afternoon, ninety minutes after the impact with the truck, he is singing the old hymn 'What a friend we have in Jesus' and suddenly there under the tarp I start signing with him. I was back on earth.

What was your first experience then? You just found yourself singing? How did you do the transition from . . .

I was in a dark zone. My last earthly memory was driving onto this large bridge on a rainy, cold day, and now I'm in the dark. And the reason I'm in the dark, I find out subsequently, is that I'm covered up with the tarp because they have covered up this hideously mangled body. And this man is under the tarp praying for me—I don't know who he is. So I was very confused and puzzled by what was happening. I sensed no pain because, as you might imagine, my body was still in shock. I didn't really know what had happened. I didn't know that the truck had hit me, I didn't know why I was singing and I certainly didn't know who this voice was praying for me.

Dick prayed for you obediently. But are you happy that he brought you back? That would have been a bit of a mixed blessing.

It was to be a very mixed blessing over the next few weeks, months and years. Obviously it was an incredible miracle that I survived this accident. I was dismembered; my left leg was just basically . . . I lost four inches of femur—the largest bone in the human body. My left arm was in the back seat of the car; my right leg was crushed, impaled on the steering wheel. The roof of the car had crushed my head so I was in such a hideous condition.

The accident happened at 11.45 am. I didn't get to the level-one trauma centre in Houston, Texas, until 6.16 pm. Six-and-a-half hours passed before I'm in the hospital. Dick had prayed that I wouldn't have any brain damage or internal injuries and all the previous tests indicated that I had both of them; and when I got to the hospital after Dick's prayer I didn't have either one of them.

I was in an ICU for two weeks, in a hospital bed for thirteen months and I had thirty-four major operations. I was told I would never walk again. I do today. So many, many miracles happened. But it was a very, very long haul for me to be able to have some kind of meaningful life after that terrible wreck.

And that recovery process continues today?
I had many years of therapy. I call it my new 'normal'. Sometimes things happen to us from which we are never the same. We have to embrace that. I know a lot of people who have gone through losses and tragedies and difficulties and their response is, like mine was for a while, bitterness. But I had to decide that I was going to be better and not bitter. I had to decide that I was going to take this mess that I found myself in and try to somehow make it a message that would help someone else.

I spend a lot of my time now trying to encourage people about how to get past life-altering—in some cases, tragic—experiences and have a meaningful life. I worked my way through that process and I'm still working my way through. I don't move the way I used to move and I don't do the things I used to do. But God has given me other things to do now, and I'm going to do the best I can to try to help other people through those experiences too.

You still live with chronic pain, don't you?
Yeah, I do. I manage it. If you don't manage it, it will manage you. I don't take any drugs, which I don't discourage if the doctor prescribes them. But for me the side effects were worse in some cases than the narcotic affect of numbing the pain. So I just work on a day-to-day basis to try to get myself through the day. I know my limitations. When you have broken everything you have, arthritis

and all those things are kind of your constant companion. So I'm going to go as long as I can and do as much as I can until the Lord takes me back home.

And there was depression and despair there too.
I had a real struggle with that. Part of it was that I didn't know why this happened to me. Of course it was an accident. The man was not trying to hit me with his truck; he just lost control. But I really struggled with the emotional, spiritual and certainly physical pain, and was mightily depressed. I hit the bottom. The only good thing I know about hitting bottom is that when you hit the bottom you have a way to push off. I really hit the bottom one night in that hospital room after months of surgery and pain and not much hope—no one could give me much hope. But I decided that I was going to take this mess and try to help somebody else through their mess, and that took the focus off me and put the focus on ministry, and that was the beginning of my recovery. I try to bring hope to people. Not only hope about eternal life and the world to come but a better life now through Christ and his constant companionship.

Sceptical minds would say, 'Look, is there any way you could have been simply concussed or something? Is there any way this experience of heaven could have been some sort of mental creation as your brain was lacking oxygen?' How do you respond to the critics?
Two observations. I hear of people who supposedly have near death experiences, and I am in the camp with the sceptics. I hear the stories and I am fascinated with them, but I discount them because in most cases they do not agree with what the Bible says about heaven. In my case they all agreed, and I found things and saw things in heaven that

I never really paid much attention to in the Bible, because it seems so far away. You read about heaven in the Bible you think, 'Well, one day I will be there.' When I came back and did an extensive study of heaven, I really found that so much of what I saw there was what the Bible said, and so much more of what the Bible said I had ignored. So for me it's the most real experience of my existence.

Secondly, that experience is now the standard by which I judge everything else. Now this world is temporal. The people of the world are temporal. They are all passing; it's passing. So I live my life in a complete reverse fashion. To me heaven was the most real experience of my entire existence. It is more real than this conversation we are having. It's more real than Australia. It's more real than anything here on earth. I still appreciate the folks that are sceptical, but I lived it. If you saw pictures of the accident, if you know what condition I was in, and you know that I was absolutely dead for ninety minutes and there is no earthly explanation for my survival, then it is more plausible. I assure you, it was real. It was absolutely real.

What have been the big enduring lessons you have taken from that experience?
God answers prayer. I am a living testimony to answered prayer. The only reason I survived is because many, many people prayed, many of them unbeknown that I was dead. I had nothing to do with my survival that day.

I also believe that God is still in the miracle business. Thousands of miraculous things had to happen for me to survive and also have any meaningful life. So I believe in miracles. It's not an Old Testament concept—God is doing miracles today.

I do believe that we can have a new life after horrible tragic circumstances and losses. And I do believe that heaven is real, and I'm going to try to get as many people to go there as I possibly can before God calls me back. Jesus said, 'I am the way, the truth and the life, no man comes to the Father except through me.' So I want to point people to the way, I want people to know the truth and I want people to have a better life now, and eternal life with Christ. Those are my lessons and that's what I preach.

Any understanding now as to why you went through this whole experience?
I'm not sure I'll ever understand it completely, especially when you see all the scars that I walk around with, but I understand it better. It's to tell people that heaven is real and try to help them have a more meaningful existence now. So many people are just pining away. They have lost their mother, their child drowned, they have lost their job, they are going through really, really difficult experiences, and they are wondering why. And the *why* is not as important as *what you do* with the things that happen to you. I try to encourage people to be better, not bitter. And it's so easy to be bitter. I was. But God has helped take my disappointment and turn it into divine appointments.

CULTURE

Culture is the sum of all the forms of art, of love, and of thought, which, in the course of centuries, have enabled man to be less enslaved.
André Malraux

The earth is the Lord's, and everything in it, the world, and all who live in it.
King David

James Morrison

James Morrison is internationally recognised as one of the crème-de-la-crème of the jazz world. He has played for world leaders and royalty, and who can forget his performance at the opening of the Sydney Olympic Games.

Ray Brown describes him as a genius; Dizzy Gillespie calls him the best of the best. And anyone who has caught one of Morrison's live shows knows he also has a wicked sense of humour. The virtuoso dropped by Open House one night and brought his trumpet with him.

You formed your first band at nine and were playing in clubs by the age of thirteen. Is that legal?
We're not sure, but it doesn't matter now does it! I think at the time we had some sort of dispensation that as I long as I stayed on the stage, quite seriously, for the whole night, and didn't go into the club proper, then I was OK because there was no licensed premises on stage. So when the band took a break they would go into the club while I stayed on stage and played a little solo piano.

Playing with Ray Charles must have been a highlight for you.
It was wonderful. We spent a few months going right around the world. When you first hear Ray Charles it is great. When you first

195

hear him live it is wonderful. When you're first on stage with him in the band it is fantastic! But I still expected, you know, that after ten nights, twenty nights, thirty nights playing with him it would wear off. But at the end of those three months he would start to sing and it would be exactly the same as the first night—oh, listen to that!

There have been others too: the BB Kings, the Dizzy Gillepsies, the George Bensons of the world. Is there any artist that you would say has been your favourite to work with, apart from, say, Ray Charles?
Oh no, I can't even say Ray is my favourite because then what do I say about Dizzy? They're all different. Ray Charles is my favourite Ray Charles. I have been really lucky to work with most of my record collection—that's how I think of it—which is just fantastic.

I often wondered what it must have been like for you doing the opening fanfare for the Sydney Olympic Games. Do you ever get nervous? Was that a moment when you did?
No, I get excited. I mean, the opening of the Games, home town, 100,000 people standing in front of you, I don't know how many more watching on TV—half a billion people or something. It doesn't get much bigger than that. But at the same time, all I had to do was blow the trumpet, which is what I do.

Nerves are an interesting thing. I know some wonderful musicians who get nervous—people who have been in the business for years. It's just part of how they are as a performer. But it's not something I have ever had to deal with.

In one way this is a silly thing to say, but in another way it is a real thing to say: if you can pick up the trumpet at home in your bedroom and play that opening fanfare, and play it correctly and not miss notes, well, it's the same trumpet and the same lips as playing in front of all those people.

But it's not the same context!
I know. What people would say is the consequences of missing something in your bedroom are small and the consequences of missing it on live television broadcast around the world at the opening of the Games—you'll never live it down. I don't want to sound egotistical; I don't want to sound like I'm *blowing my own trumpet*!

Boom, tish!
Thank you! You do the boom-tishes.

But for those consequences to be considered there has to be a possibility that you might miss the note. For me, playing is a joyful thing. I sense the gift of music and so I don't think, 'Oh, what if this goes wrong?' It won't. Not because I'm a hero but because I'm using my gift and I'm doing what I'm supposed to do, and I know I can do it. So the consequences of playing in front of people at the Olympics or in my bedroom are exactly the same.

A lot of people wish they could say that very same thing, James, with the same degree of confidence.
Confidence is an interesting thing. If your confidence is based on, 'I know I am really good; I've done a lot of practice' etc.; if I keep starting with 'I', then I'll start to feel nervous. But if your confidence is based on a belief that this is what you are supposed to be doing, this is part of what you are here for, there is this great sense of relief. I wouldn't be led to do something like this if I wasn't supposed to

be doing it. The confidence you then have is based on something bigger than you.

When did you realise that this was what you were called to do? Was there ever an epiphany moment?
I think there were . . . was an epiphany. I was going to say there were epiphanies, or 'epiphani', is it? There was never a moment when I realised that this is what I'm supposed to do. There was a moment when I realised I *could* do it. There was a moment where I decided I *wanted* to do it. I was very young and I first heard some jazz. I went, 'Oh, I want to play that!' It was a decision. Rather than having a moment you sort of go, 'Gee, I'm probably supposed to be doing this because it's kind of working out well.' Then over the years there's more of a gentle but deeper realisation: I know why I wanted to and I know why I could—because I'm *supposed* to.

What was the first song you mastered?
You're assuming I have mastered one! The first song I learned to play that I recall was . . . want a sample?

Please.
[Plays 'Mary Had a Little Lamb']
    I could teach you that one.
    [Laughter]
    But the real song that I remember learning was the 'Basin Street Blues'.
    [Plays]

Absolutely beautiful.
That was the first jazz piece that I heard, so naturally it was the first I wanted to play.

Music has such an ability to change moods. Do you think it can go even deeper and affect the spirit in some way?
Absolutely. Not only can it—it does. And I think there are a couple of reasons for that. I'm an avid reader; I love words and I love reading. Written things can move you and touch you deeply, but there is one difference between words and music. There is an intellect thing that must take place when I read words. First I have to do the reading; secondly I have to understand the words, the sentence; and then with comprehension this wonderful dawning of the meaning happens.

But music bypasses that whole first process. If I play music to you, you don't need to understand it. You don't even need to know what I'm playing. You certainly don't need to know the notes, like you need to know the letters in the words. You don't have to understand the form of the song, like a sentence. You can just sit there and let the music happen to you. It speaks to you emotionally, directly, without involving your intellect.

A musician is not someone who can play the trumpet. That's not a musician, that's a trumpeter. A musician is someone who can take a feeling and turn it into musical sounds. So not only can music move your emotions and create moods (that is more of a surface thing), but it can become a spiritual thing. I am feeling something. That is one of the things about music.

People over the years have talked about what is good and what is bad music. When most people have that conversation they are talking about taste. When someone says, 'Oh, that rock 'n' roll is awful music', what they mean is 'I don't like it'. Here is the thing that I think makes 'good' music or not: not what genre it is, but what feeling did I have. If I have a feeling that I want to convey to you that we would generally accept as a good feeling, something positive, then provided I can convey it to you, that is good music.

That leads us to the Gospel Collections *you've released, now two albums. If music can touch us spiritually, could the Gospel genre, its meaning, form and the very essence of its lyrics, go deeper still?*
I would say it focuses the message more. If I play with a general joy of being alive, of the gift of life and of knowing my spiritual place in the universe, and I play the 'Basin Street Blues', it will be a wonderful feeling and you will get it. You will feel that joy.

But if I specifically focus the message more than just that general joy, and I want to talk about something the church celebrates and I pick a hymn, it doesn't matter if I turn it into a jazz number or not. If I pick a hymn and you know what that hymn means, now I have focused the message. Perhaps rather than saying it goes deeper, I'd say it becomes more potent, like anything does when it's focused.

Well, that trumpet is gathering dust at the moment.
Yes, it's been down there for nearly two-and-a-half minutes now!

What about a track off the latest Gospel Collections *album. Can you do something like 'Oh Happy Day?'*
I can play a little bit of 'Oh Happy Day'.
    [Plays]

Let's talk about some of the deeper aspects of your life then. You're the son of a Methodist preacher . . .
Yes.

What was growing up a preacher's kid like for you?
Well, it was interesting in the fact that everything revolved around the church. With dad being the minister, there'd be various things going on at home, people coming over and him ministering to them. Bible study class would be in our lounge room, and so would choir practice. And living in the parsonage right behind the church in a country town meant that most of our time was spent there. To a young boy this was both a blessing and a curse.

The blessing was that it meant that church was part of life; it wasn't just this thing that happened on one day. There are all sorts of good sides to that, not the least of which was, with dad being the minister, it was like going to work with your dad every week.

The curse to a young lad like me was exactly the same—everything revolved around the church. So if you wanted to do something else with your friends on Sunday, just forget it. You cannot *not* turn up to church when your dad is the minister.

Did you feel pressure to live up to being the 'minister's kid'?
Oh yes. You would be looked at like that, and if a teacher wanted to bring you into line in class they would say, 'I didn't expect that from *you*'. [Laughter] 'I don't think your father would be very happy to hear about *this*,' and that sort of thing. So that was the drag. Why can't my dad be, you know, working down at the railroad or something?

Some people who grow up in that environment feel the need to break away when they get older. Did you ever rebel?
It wasn't so much that I needed to get away because, as you've already said, from the age of thirteen I was playing in night clubs.

That must have been a scandal in the church.
Well, I was looked on as an evangelist! But by the time I got to church on Sunday morning I had just spent Friday and Saturday playing at night clubs, so there was nothing to break free from. I was out there.

No, it was a different feeling. [Christianity] had always been such a part of life that it wasn't special. It wasn't like someone who goes to church and has this epiphany or suddenly realises the whole thing. It was just a given, so in a way it was familiarity making it less special.

So was there a personal moment of commitment for you to the person of Jesus?
Yes, but again, maybe because of being the preacher's kid, it wasn't just once. You'd have this realisation and commitment and it wasn't that you fell by the wayside, you were still there, but then it would come again, and you'd realise it all over again, but stronger or in a new light. In fact, when I was nineteen, when I was well and truly a jazz musician—I'd been touring with Don Burrows and his band for three years—imagine what it was like when I came out with, 'I know what I want to be. I'm going to be a preacher!'

[Laughter]

Even people like mum and dad who should've been delighted said, 'Are you sure that's a good idea?' Because they could see that my ministry was in music. But I did a lay preacher's course and started preaching Sunday nights.

What was your first message on?
My first message was directed to my peers, the teenagers, and it was along the lines that anyone who is seventeen or eighteen thinks they know everything, and that perhaps we didn't. Perhaps there were

others that knew more than us, particularly if we bothered to look in the Bible. So that was the first message.

Then there was a gradual realisation that I could actually do a whole lot more with a trumpet in my hands. I have to say, without *blowing my own trumpet . . .* That's where your boom-tish thing comes in . . .

Boom, tish!
. . . that I thought I was pretty good in the pulpit.

The problem was that nobody else did!
[Laughter]
I had a bit of a gift of the gab. But no, there is a reason why people become so affected when I play.

There really is a difference between somebody who has just learnt to plonk out some notes on the piano, and somebody who really is gifted.
The very fact that you have learnt it and that you are 'plonking them out' is quite descriptive, as in it's mostly for the person playing. You know what I mean? You plonk out a tune because you enjoy it. The common instrument for that is the guitar, because it's portable and you can take it to a party or take it camping, pull it out and play. What is that for? It's for the person who is playing it and perhaps their friends around them. It's not for the world.

When you are given a gift of much more musicality than that, then it is not for you. I don't actually need to hear the trumpet. Playing trumpet, in my case, is for everybody else—so that they can hear it too. I don't create the music. I wouldn't be so presumptuous. I'm the person whom the music comes through, so that everyone else can hear it.

How would you describe your faith these days?
Now there's an interesting question. How does one describe
something like that . . .

*Would you describe your relationship with God in relational terms, like
a father and a son, or a friend to a friend? You can take some time over
this if you like; play a little mood music in the background.*
[Laughter]

I'd have to begin answering that question by saying I don't
describe it in my own mind. It is not something for description.
I wouldn't liken it to other relationships, and one of the reasons for
that is that all of those things for me start to place limits on it in
my mind. As soon as I can describe it, I'm boxing it in.

I look around at the creation and I say, 'Well, there isn't any part
of this that isn't part of God.' Because if I can go to a dreadful slum
somewhere, or where there is a war, and say that God's not here,
that God didn't make this bit, then who did?

The creation, which is everything, is made by God. That doesn't
mean that God wants a war to be happening; that's not what I'm
saying. I'm saying it's all part of the creation, and in the same sort
of way my relationship has to be as all-encompassing as that; the
bad days, the good days, the frustrations, as well as the joys and
the ecstasies.

Like anyone else, I want to define things. I want to understand
them. But I have a bit of a theory that the really important
things shouldn't be defined; they shouldn't be intellectualised or
understood. A scientist can tell us stuff about quantum physics and
the quantum dynamics level—stuff that I've been reading about
lately. But let's say, OK, let's have a quick talk about love now. What
have we got? What measurements have we got? Forget it. There is

no proof that it even exists and there never will be, because as soon as you can prove it you can define it and you can limit it, and it's unlimited. So, I've got a feeling that anything I can prove, describe, define, automatically means it's not that important.

Tell me about modal playing.
Ah, we're going to talk about modal playing, are we?

I remember the first time I saw you and your brother play. I was in Melbourne, it must have been 1997. Merryn and I were just married and were driving through and you were playing at the Myer Music Bowl. It was a great concert. You remember that one?
You were in about the fourth row, weren't you?

I waved and you waved back.
Yeah, thirty-sixth in from the left.

You called the guards and said take him out!
[Laughter]

I think that was when you were talking about this ability to both blow and breathe at the same time.
Oh, you mean circular breathing.

That's what I mean. Give us an example of that.
This is how you play a didgeridoo, of course.

Can anybody do that or only certain people?
Oh, anyone can once you learn how. You breathe in your nose and out your mouth at the same time. The way to learn is quite simple.

You grab a straw and a glass of water and blow some bubbles gently. Just start blowing gently, and while you are blowing try and take a breath through your nose. That's a much better way than actually telling you what to do with the valve in your throat and everything. Just try it. You will find that you will snatch a breath and the first time you do it maybe the bubbles will stop. Just concentrate on keeping the bubbles going, look at them and snatch a breath through your nose, just quickly. You will find you will do it and the bubbles won't stop. You are using circular breathing.

Now to take that to the level where you can do it playing a trumpet, which takes a lot more air, is harder, but the technique is the same. Of course, be careful doing this because if you do it backwards you will drown.

[Laughter]

He's full of jokes tonight, isn't he—that's what comes from being a preacher's kid.
Exactly. But it's very handy, not just for playing the trumpet or any other wind instrument, but blowing up balloons at kids' parties; it saves a lot of time not having to stop to take a breath!

So you can keep a note going literally for hours.
Well, until your lips or whatever can't vibrate. Something else would run out. I've never found out because I've never wanted to listen to it for that long. Neither does anyone else.

Give us an example.
I will but what the listeners will hear is just a note going on and on; they won't see what is happening. Trust me, I have no apparatus connected to the trumpet—this is just me.

[Plays a continuous note]

It sounds like they've got the test pattern on or something. That can go on for a very long time.

How long did it take you to master that?

It just happened one night. I was playing a passage and running out of breath and I couldn't let go of the note. It was just all wrong to stop the note at that point in the song. I thought, 'I'll just grab a quick breath.' I wasn't even really thinking—how can you without the note stopping—and I snatched a breath. Afterwards I went, wait a minute, the note didn't stop! I did it again and thought, 'This is good; I don't have to stop for breaths any more.'

We are a covering a lot of things tonight!

We are! Yeah, it's quite educational . . . Um, I've totally forgotten the next question I was going to ask you.

If you're listening right now and you're wondering what is going on, Sheridan has completely lost it, and knows not what to ask me next.

I had this great question for you . . .

While he is looking for the question, I will just play something.

[Plays randomly]

Have you worked out the next question yet?

My question was, would you like to take us out with one last song from the Gospel Collections *album?*

Have you got something in mind? Do you have the album handy? Would you believe that I made the album and chose the songs, and I can't tell you what's on it?

Well 'Nobody Knows the Trouble I've Seen' is quite a nice one.
Why don't I play a bit of it live here in the studio, just solo trumpet
which, of course, is missing all the drums, bass, guitar and vocals,
and you could even, with the magic of the studio, morph into a
bit of the actual track.
    [Plays]

*Beautiful stuff. And every window in the studio has got a crack in it
now. Thanks very much, James Morrison.*
Thanks, mate.

Katherine Paterson

IF IT'S NOT A GOOD BOOK, IT'S NOT GOOD ENOUGH
FOR CHILDREN

Katherine Paterson's enthralling tales have tickled the imagination of countless children. Books like *Come Sing, Jimmy Jo*; *The Great Gilly Hopkins*; *Flip-Flop Girl*, and the acclaimed *Bridge to Terabithia* have earned her over one hundred awards and recognitions, twelve honorary degrees and a legion of fans worldwide. *Bridge to Terabithia* has twice now been adapted for the screen.

As a child Katherine Paterson never wanted to write. In fact, she wanted to become either a movie star or a missionary. Katherine's childhood dreams, creative practices, personal beliefs and more flowed forth in what became a most delightful Open House discussion.

Those two childhood aspirations of movie star or missionary seem poles apart. What appealed to you about both?
Well, I think it might indicate that I was a crazy little mixed up kid! Of course, my parents were missionaries in China, so that was the world I grew up in. And I loved acting and I loved the imagination, so after I'd seen a few movies I thought, 'Oh my, wouldn't that be wonderful!'

Let's talk about your time in China—the place of your birth. Your parents were missionaries in the 1930s, weren't they?
Yeah, they went out in 1923. I was born in 1932, which tells you exactly how old I will be on October 31!

Our friends listening are doing the mathematics right now. How old were you when you left China?
We were actually evacuated twice. We left in 1938 when the war between China and Japan really began, and we returned in 1939. And then at the end of 1940 the American consulate decided that the United States and Japan would be at war within a short time, so we were once again evacuated. I was eight years old the second time I was evacuated.

That's quite a bit of to-ing and fro-ing for a young girl.
It was very hard for me because you were always moving and making a new life in a new place. I think that's maybe one reason why I became a great reader as a child and entertained myself with my own imagination, because when you're in a new place you don't have friends. You have to make up your own games.

When did your siblings come along?
I was the middle child of five. I had an older brother and an older sister and two younger sisters.

Even with that number of siblings it sounds like life was still a bit of a lonely existence for you.
Well, my older brother and sister were very close, and my two younger sisters were several years younger than I and they were close. So I was sort of in the middle.

Is it true that your first language was actually Chinese?
Yes. We lived in a compound but everybody else who lived behind our gate was Chinese. So although our parents spoke English to us, everybody else spoke Chinese to us. There's a letter from my father to his mother when I'm about two years old and it sounds as though my lovely, quiet father, who only spoke when he had something valuable to say, is a little puzzled as to what to do with this child who won't shut up in two languages.

You said that those early experiences could well be the reason you went into the seclusion of books and into the world of the imagination. Did it shape you in any other ways?
Well, I think it's very valuable to be bilingual early on. It does something very valuable to your brain. You just have to think in different ways—if you're thinking in Chinese you think a certain way and if you think in English you're thinking in another way, and I think it's a valuable birthright to have.

So you move to the United States in your eighth year of life. Describe life in the US.
At first it was very, very hard for me because I was a foreigner and wore strange clothes, spoke with a strange accent and came from somewhere 'over there'. Of course, American children didn't have a very strong sense of geography, so after the war with Japan began they concluded that I was one of 'them'. That first year or so was very, very difficult for me.

The library was the sanctuary for me. There was a wonderful library in the North Carolina school where I was and the librarian, as I remember, was a very nurturing sort of person. She just introduced me to all kinds of wonderful books, and that's where my friends were in those early years.

The books were your friends.
Yeah, the books were my friends.

Which books most impacted you during those years?
There was a woman who was actually Hungarian and immigrated to America; her name was Kate Seredy. She wrote about Hungary and yet the heroine of her books was a child of war who had gone into the country—very much like how I felt. I loved those books.

One of the books that I truly loved and that certainly influenced me, which I think I read before I left China actually, was *The Secret Garden* by Frances Hodgson Burnett. There again it's about an expatriate child who has a terrible temper—which I also had!—who is given the key to a secret garden. It gave me a lot of hope as a child that things might look up for me and there might be a magical world for me.

Did things look up for you during your teenage years?
Absolutely, absolutely—not when I was a teenager but by the time I had finished elementary school, because we were able to stay at the same school for a little over three years, and by the time I was in the seventh grade I had friends and was not regarded as weird, as I had initially been.

Then we moved again. I went to a different school in the eighth grade, two different schools in the ninth grade, two different schools in eleventh grade, and so the teenage years were very hard. But even moving as much as I did, in my teenage years I was able to have some close friends that weren't necessarily living in a book—actual living people! That made a huge difference to me.

You may not have become a movie star as you'd hoped during childhood, but you did become a missionary in Japan.
I did. If anyone had told me when I was nine years old that I would go and live in Japan for four years I wouldn't have believed them for a minute. The Japanese I knew were soldiers, they were the enemy, and I was very frightened because we lived in occupied China for that one year. In one place that we lived the soldiers would come and question my parents, and my mother always served tea to them in a very polite way, but I found them very frightening. Another place we lived was near the beach, up north, and they were practising manoeuvres in our yard—beach landings right in our yard. When the war first began we were caught in a place where there was a lot of bombing going on, so it was a frightening few early years.

I never would have gone to Japan except that when I was in seminary I met a Japanese woman pastor who became a good friend, and she persuaded me that if I would give Japanese people a chance I would come to love them. She was absolutely right. Even more than that I came to understand what it meant to be loved by people that you thought you hated. I think everyone should have that experience. It really changes the way that you look at life.

As missionaries your parents were obviously strong Christians. When would you say your own personal Christian faith began?
I'm sure it began from my very earliest years—being a Presbyterian, we baptise babies! It's been a growing process. I think there were times when I was a teenager when I had the usual questions that teenagers have and thought that if God existed at all then he wasn't

loving. I had a very good older friend, a woman, who introduced me to C.S. Lewis at that time, which was extremely helpful for me and really helped shape the rest of my theological thinking. I'm very grateful for that.

I can see the influences there, from a wonderfully imaginative writer as well.
Yes, yes. People ask me where the word 'Terabithia' came from. I really thought I had made it up and then I was rereading *The Voyage of the Dawn Treader* and realised that there's an island there called 'Terabinthia'. I thought, 'Oh I've pinched it! I've got to change it!' Oh no, no, no—Lewis pinched it from the Bible: the terebinth tree in the Bible. So if he pinches from the Bible, then I can pinch from him.

[Laughter]

But there is definitely influence from Lewis in Terabithia.

Tell us about your four years in Japan as a missionary—what you were doing and how you were changed through that experience.
Because Japanese is such an extremely difficult language, the Presbyterian Church sent you to language school for two years. I taught some English Bible classes and things like that, but mostly I was just trying to make my way in Japanese language.

Then after those two years I was asked to go to the island of Shikoku and I became sort of a Christian education assistant to eleven rural pastors. I went from church to church and did whatever the pastor felt would be most helpful. In one church I taught the Bible in English, for high school students who were trying to learn English. In another church I taught the Bible in Japanese for the whole community. Everybody came. It was way in the country and most of them had never even seen an American, so I was a great curiosity at that point. Some of the churches wanted me to preach and others wanted me to help the church school teachers with methods of teaching the Bible and teaching children.

It did change me because I was a single woman, quite young, and in each of the churches they felt they had to really take care of me. It was a very close and wonderful relationship for me. I really, truly loved being there and I loved the people that I worked with.

Why did you leave?

In our denomination, after four years you're given a year back at home, and I was given a fellowship to do further graduate work at Union Seminary in New York City. It was during that year that I met John Paterson. So although I had planned to go back to Japan, he sort of changed those plans. That was when I got married, had four children in four years and started writing.

How would you describe your faith these days?

It's sort of hard to talk about—to look at your insides and express them for other people. I think it has grown. I think it's less grabby, if you know what I mean. I used to feel like I needed to hold on very much to the tenets of belief. Now, although the tenets of belief are important to me, relationship with God, with prayer, reading the Bible for myself—not to use it as a law or guide stick but just to enrich my spirit and to come to know God better—that's what's really important.

I think in some ways my faith is quieter and deeper than it has been. But then I'm seventy-five years old now, and I think it changes as you grow older. I think my faith has made me much more inclusive. I was more exclusive as a younger person, but now

I see the great amazing grace of God for the *whole* world and I'm just so grateful for knowing that and for wanting the world to know it.

Let's move into your writing years. You get married, have four children in four years, and begin your writing career.
Actually I started writing because the Presbyterian Church that had given [me] this study fellowship asked me to write a book for fifth and sixth graders to use in church curriculum. I felt I owed it to them for giving me that year of study. I wrote the book for them and realised how much I enjoyed writing. So I thought, 'I've got all these little children, I'm not going to go back to school teaching or anything, I think I'll write.'

I wrote for seven years. During those seven years I sold only one short story, and the little Roman Catholic magazine that bought it folded the following month! I sold one poem to another very tiny Roman Catholic magazine that stopped publication before they published my poem.

So it wasn't a roaring success from the beginning!
Yeah, great success! Then finally I began to write a book set in twelfth-century Japan. It was turned down a number of times, but was finally picked out of the slush pile of unsolicited manuscripts by a young woman who truly liked it. She took it to the senior editor and it so happened that the senior editor had just returned from a trip to Japan and was excited by the idea of American young people knowing more about feudal Japan. So they published it. I was very fortunate because the editor to whom I was assigned in 1970 is still my editor today.

Really?
Yeah. She's edited all of my novels; nearly everything I've written. I've written some books for other companies, but Virginia Buckley has edited almost everything I've written.

It's rare that a writer would have a relationship with an editor for thirty-odd years.
Very rare; very rare in this day and time.

Let's talk about perhaps your best-known book, Bridge to Terabithia. *You based it on some events in your own life, didn't you?*
Well, as a seven and eight-year-old, our son David's best friend was a girl named Lisa Hill. I was a little worried that his best friend was a girl, but I shouldn't have been. She was bright and imaginative and quite the tomboy. She was the only girl who would play on the boy's ball team. The summer after they had both turned eight years old Lisa was vacationing with her family on the beach, and was struck and killed by lightning. It was such a horrible event that I was trying to make sense out of something that didn't make any sense for me.

As a writer and a storyteller you know that a story has to make sense. It has a beginning, a middle and an end, and when you get to the end, even if intellectually it doesn't make sense, emotionally it's got to make sense for you. So I tried to write a story to make sense of something that didn't make any sense. That was how I wrote *Bridge to Terabithia.*

It's David who decided he wanted to turn it into a movie. For a long time nobody wanted to make a movie from a children's book. Then there were people who were saying, 'Well, OK, but can't we just hurt her a little bit, or break her leg or something, or let her go into a coal mine?' The idea of killing one of the leads was just so abhorrent. But David was determined that it would be done with integrity, not only because it was his mother's book but because he wanted to honour his friend.

How did David deal with the loss of Lisa back then?
Very poorly. It was almost more than you could ask an eight-year-old boy to deal with. One of the worst things for me happened one night when I was putting David into his bed and saying his prayers. He said, 'Now I know why Lisa died.' I said, 'What do you mean?' 'Well,' he said, 'it wasn't because Lisa was bad, it was because I'm bad. So God killed Lisa and then he's going to kill me, and he's going to kill you, and he's going kill daddy and he's going kill Lynne, and then he's going kill John . . .' He just went down the list of everybody he loved that God was going to kill because he was such a bad little boy. Now I promise you, that is *not* the God we sought to teach our children!

He was just trying to make sense out of it too. I mean, it made no sense to him that his friend who was good and wonderful should be struck and killed by lightning. He was trying desperately in his eight-year-old way to make some sense out of it.

Ultimately, what meaning did you find in Lisa's death?
I'm not even sure that I can articulate it. I think that through the years when I've seen, sadly, the influence of the book and how much the book has meant, that has sort of become the meaning—which is a terrible thing to say, because I don't think that Lisa died in order that this book be born.

No, of course not.
But I think that good can be brought out of tragedy and evil, and I think a lot of good has come. And I've been very grateful that Lisa's family has seemed to feel that way about it too. As tragic and as awful as her death was—and they are still not over her death; you never get over the death of a child—they are grateful that the books have spoken to people around the world.

When you were writing Bridge to Terabithia *you were actually suffering from cancer as well, is that right?*
That's right. When I got to the chapter when Leslie Burke was going to die, I just stopped writing; that was the only way I could keep her alive. Then, this good friend of mine from seminary that lived in the same town asked me over lunch how my book was coming along. She didn't know what book I was writing or anything, she was just making conversation. 'Well,' I said, 'I'm trying to write this book about a friendship between a boy and a girl in which the girl dies. And I just can't let her die. I can't go through Lisa's death again.' She said, 'I don't think it's Lisa's death you can't face. I think it's yours.' Then I realised she was right and that I had to finish the book, because I had to face my own death. We all do.

That would've been hard. How did you write the next chapter?
With sweat pouring down my arms!
   [Laughter]

Not just the inspiration but the perspiration, as they say.
Yes, exactly.

Unlike other young adult authors of the time, you touched on these themes of death and jealousy in your work, and that made you a little controversial. You could've written a nice children's book that didn't incorporate those kinds of things. Why were they important to raise for young readers?

Well, I was a child, and I know how very deeply children feel. I often say that I don't have that good a memory for events but I do have good memory for emotions. I know how deeply children feel. I think that children ask very deep questions and that we as adults tend to dismiss this, and we don't want to think that our children feel deeply because we don't want them to hurt. But I think by not taking their questions seriously and not taking their deepest feelings seriously—whether they're of fear, grief, anger or jealously—we do them an enormous disservice. I think the reason children like my books is because I take them seriously, and I take their hard questions and the hard things they have to deal with in life seriously.

I often say that the reason I'm suited to write for children is because I ask the same questions children ask. And they're the important questions. I think as we get older our questions get less important because we think there's no answer, and so we stop struggling with the really big questions.

Over the years you must've received some really interesting letters from your young readers. Do any stand out as most memorable?
Well, I had a wonderful experience . . . I'd like to tell you about the nice ones, is that all right?

Why not.
This was some years ago. I was out in California autographing and this very tall, good-looking young man came to the table where

I was writing and said, 'I'm sure you don't remember me, but my name is Kevin and I wrote you many years ago.' I replied that I hoped I'd answered him. He said, 'Oh yes, you did. I wrote that I had leukaemia and that my babysitter, who I was very close to, had died very suddenly and that someone gave me a copy of *Bridge to Terabithia* and it meant so much to me that I wrote you a letter.'

He said, 'I still have your letter.'

And I said, 'Kevin, I still have yours.'

Isn't that beautiful.
And another letter, more recently, that has meant a great deal to me was from a young National Guardsman who was stationed in Afghanistan. He was lonely and frightened. His wife sent him a copy of *Bridge to Terabithia* and he wrote this absolutely wonderful letter about how going around the city in his weaponry, all he could think about was the beauty of my book.

How old was he?
He was in his twenties. I've since gotten to meet him and we've gotten to be friends.

It shows that great children's literature doesn't have to be limited to children.
My feeling is that if it's not a good book it's not good enough for children.

[Laughter]

What would you like your writing to accomplish?
I think everybody wants me to say that I have message that I want to give. But I think readers get to choose their own messages.

222

Every reader is going to come with a different life experience, with different abilities and different imaginations and they'll read the book differently; what they learn from the book is going to be different and what the book means to each reader will be different. If the writer starts out with a message or an answer, it's propaganda. I've written propaganda. I hope it was good propaganda! But a story is many faceted; it really is the writer's exploration of a question, and so what the meaning is and what the answers are are really for the reader to discover.

OK, Katherine, we need to give those budding writers hanging on your every word some tips on how to do the craft of writing.
I think reading is the most helpful thing you can do. I think that was my best preparation for being a writer. I was such a reader, and I'm still such a reader. I really think of myself as more of a reader than a writer, even today. Even if you read things that aren't of the highest quality you still learn how sentences are put together and how the language works and how a story works, and I think you just absorb it.

And of course it helps to write. So many people tell me they'll write when they have time. I just look at them, because when I began writing I had all these little children and I wrote in five minute snatches. It wasn't for years that I had this luxury of a whole uninterrupted *hour* to write.

So I often say to people, do fifteen minutes of writing a day then at the end of the year you will have a book. Your subconscious keeps working even when you're doing other things.

I think it's not so much time that people lack, but nerve. It takes a lot of nerve to write a book and put it out for the world to see. I said to my son David, who's the writer in the family (although his brother John is getting a book published next year), I said, 'You've got plenty of talent, but the world is full of people with talent. You've got to have perseverance too. If you have both talent and perseverance you will probably make it.'

And are there things we can do to nurture the imagination and the creative abilities we have?
Yes. I think all of the arts are going to nurture your imagination and creativity. I've been taking pastel painting lessons for several years because it's another way of seeing imaginatively that words alone don't do for you. Music is a great help too.

Living a broad life, in many ways?
Yes, yes.

Exploring the richness of God's good creation.
Absolutely.

Marina Prior

Frequently referred to as Australia's 'leading lady' of musical theatre, Marina Prior has played front-stage roles in some of the world's finest productions: *Camelot, Cats, West Side Story, Les Misérables* and *Phantom of the Opera*. She's done TV, recorded albums and sung alongside Jose Carreras and other great voices of our time. A sophisticated artist, Marina's performance gifts are paired with a heart for the developing world.

When she joined us on Open House, a delightful discussion evolved about her early beginnings, her clear sense of identity and her journey to Christian faith. While Marina receives many an accolade, she has that wonderful grace of not taking herself too seriously—as you'll quickly discover.

Let's be honest, Marina—while you've performed in all these big productions, the role that really launched you to fame, the role that really catapulted you into the public consciousness, was when you stepped in for Nicky Buckley on Sale of the Century.
[Laughter]
Well, that's right! That was my defining moment, Sheridan.

It was Nicky back then, wasn't it?
It was Nicky. She had gone to have a baby and they brought in a few guest presenters. I'd forgotten all about that.

Which probably means it wasn't quite the defining moment of your life.
No, possibly not. But it was a bit of fun.

Cats, Les Mis, Phantom—*that's just a few of the many roles you've had. And it all began busking on Melbourne's Bourke Street, didn't it?*
It did. I was at university studying a music degree, majoring in singing, and I didn't get that much opportunity to perform— something that I loved to do. So I used to busk in the Bourke Street Mall. More than anything else, I did it just to gain experience singing in front of people. I used to compete with trams going past me, but it was a wonderfully fun thing to do.

Did you have any nerves? You would've been a teenager then, I guess.
No, I loved it too much. And I still do. It's interesting—a lot of my colleagues suffer from nerves, but I really don't have opening night terror.

What a gift.
Oh yeah. And I'm very grateful for it and a little bemused by it. But I just love what I'm doing way too much.

How old were you when you realised you had to sing?
I was probably about six—really young. I remember when I was a tiny kid going to my mum and dad and saying that I was going to be a singer when I grew up. They sort of went, 'Of course you are, darling.'

But I always knew that was what I wanted to do. I had this inherent knowledge that that was my destiny, which sounds a bit funny. I truly believed that somehow that's what was going to happen. I didn't know *how* I was going to do it. But I've always thought that a singer is actually part of who I am. It's not just what I do.

Singing is woven into your DNA.
Yeah. It really is and it always has been. Some of my earliest memories are sitting by myself in a corner singing Seekers songs. Some of your listeners won't even know who they are! It was a long time ago.

Back then, of course, you would've been so 'with it' doing Seekers songs.
Exactly. I just haven't moved on enough, have I!

Did you have any idea back then that you might go into the more operatic or theatrical side of things rather than being a rock or pop star?
It became apparent that I didn't have a rock 'n' roll voice quite early on. Because when I was fifteen or sixteen I used to sing with a few garage bands . . .

Have you got any demo tapes?
No, no. I don't think tape recorders were invented then! But I really had this affinity with Kate Bush, because she was the one person who sang in my key. So I thought I was going to be the next Kate Bush or Linda Ronstadt.

So, you sang 'Wuthering Heights'?
Oh, I absolutely did. That was one of my busking hits.
   [Laughter]

I didn't really know what sort of singer I was going to be. Then as I went to university I kind of expected I might be an opera singer, and then music theatre sort of found me.

What was the step from singing to the theatre?
Well, during my second year in uni I was sitting with a group of friends in the cafeteria. They were all music and drama students. We were looking in the paper, having a coffee, and there was a full-page ad saying 'Chorus Wanted' for the new Broadway production of *Pirates of Penzance* that was coming to Melbourne by the Victoria State Opera. None of us had ever been for a real, professional audition before. So we all decided to go along to what was called the 'cattle call', which is, like, hundreds of people penned into that under-the-stage area, like a group of cattle. You were given a number and called up in groups of five, and then you had to step forward and sing. I just fell in love with being backstage: the smells, the sights, the sounds and the atmosphere. I took my number, stepped forward; there was an elimination process and it just kept going and going, and I ended up getting the leading role.

It must have felt really special being in that environment and thinking, 'I click with this.'
You know, it was. I remember being backstage and it was all those sort of romantic visions that I'd had about being in a theatre: it was so dusty, and there really were little light globes around the mirrors. There was the fly tower, the wings and the sand bags and ropes and bits of old props and sets shoved up the back. I thought it was the most wonderful, wonderful place. And as I was standing backstage there I had this sense, 'I've come home. I belong here.'

What a telling statement. So then you start getting cast into all of these roles—a lot of 'good girl' roles. I heard that at one stage you thought you should try a 'bad girl' role as well.

Yes. I think if you're a soprano you tend to get cast as the heroine, because you have a sweet, high voice. Typically, writers will make the romantic heroine—the good girl with all the redeeming features—the soprano. Which is fine. There are some wonderful, fascinating, dramatic journeys that a lot of those characters go on. But about six or seven years ago I was asked to play another good girl in *Guys and Dolls*. And I asked if I could play the brassy blonde—the comic role. Everybody was sort of aghast saying, 'What are you doing? Marina Prior doesn't play brassy blondes!' But I had a desire to push my boundaries and push my own perception of what I could do. I wanted to step into the danger zone a bit and go where I hadn't been tested. So I got this comic role, and since then it's been predominantly character roles and comic roles 'against type', as it's called—cast against my normal suitability.

That's interesting. So many people talk today about performers being 'brands'—a musician, artist or actor becoming like a product. And brands, by their very nature, have a very defined set of values and characteristics.

Haven't they, yeah.

I'm not sure if that's the best way to go; it really can push us into a little corner. But here you are breaking out of that and saying, 'Actually, I can do much more than that.'

I think for a long time, yeah, I did have a brand. I was sort of the romantic pre-Raphaelite heroine, gazing up into the lights and singing winsomely about some wonderful thing in a very high voice.

228

That is great and I've got a lot to be thankful for. I guess having a brand, as we say today—a type or a look—does tend to pigeonhole you. You start to stay within your own expectations of what you can do. I think life is a bit more exciting than that. I like the idea of being able to really push boundaries and morph into different characters all the time. That is the beauty of being an actor.

Well, back in the Sale of the Century *days . . .*
[Laughter]

. . . you also had a bit of time on TV. You had a special role created for you in the series GP. Would you ever go back to TV?
Certainly. I love acting and that was actually a precursor to doing these sorts of character roles. The character I played was blind, but was very unpleasant; she was awful, very selfish, very mean. She was sort of physically blind and emotionally and spiritually blind as well. I really enjoyed the challenge of doing that.

Sure, I'd do TV again if it came along. I'm not one of these people who are desperately waiting to find out what the next job is. I like to see what comes along and assess it. Nowadays I don't run after my career like I used to.

I would imagine more people are approaching you these days.
I guess so. I just don't have that desperate ambition that I used to have. That doesn't mean that I don't always want to be better than I was the day before, but in our industry there is a lot of driving ambition. Sometimes people are clinging and grasping so desperately in this industry that they're actually not being the best they can be. When opportunities come along it tends to work better if you hold them with an open hand rather than with a clenched fist.

There's the Marina Prior philosophy of success. Write it down, folks!
I might write it down too. What did I say?

[Laughter]

Let's talk about your Christian faith. You didn't grow up in a Christian family, did you?
No, not at all. It's interesting as I have since found out that I have a long Christian heritage in my family. Even the origins of my name, Prior—a priory is a church and so a Prior family was a church family. But neither of my parents were Christians. They used to drop my brother and me off at Sunday school when we were kids in the 1970s because that's what you did. It was like a babysitting service on Sunday mornings. Dad used to go back home and mow the lawn.

Some of my earliest memories are of a dear older lady with a big felt board—you know, with those felt figures—telling stories about the parables and about Jesus. Even as a tiny child it rang true. I was drawn to it; I wanted to know more about it. I discovered a great hunger for it and used to love going to Sunday school. Through that church I became a member of GFS—the Girls' Friendly Society—which my husband always laughs at. It was like Girl Guides but was a church thing. Then I went on a Christian camp to a place called Mill Valley Ranch and there I made a decision at the age of ten or eleven to follow Christ.

It's very hard when you don't have fellowship. As I got older I didn't have youth groups. We moved away and I didn't have a church to go to. The environment of this camp where I became a Christian was very spiritually alive, and when we moved I remember taking myself along at the age of about thirteen to the local church, and it was a dry old place. It was like God's waiting room. Everyone was about eighty except for me, and no one really spoke to me. And I remember thinking, 'Where is that Christianity that I experienced?' I couldn't understand why they were so completely different.

So, as the parable says, I think I had a lot of weeds growing up choking my faith. As I got older there was peer group pressure; I discovered boys, I discovered music, I discovered all sorts of things and Christian faith ceased to be cool. Isn't that sad? Because now I know so many places where my kids can go, where their faith is hugely cool, hugely empowering and life-giving for them, and they're in a great environment where they can really get deep seeds sown into them.

By the time I got to university I was in a very secular environment studying the arts, music and drama—which tends to be, if anything, very left and perhaps Buddhist and New Age-y. It was incredibly uncool to be a Christian.

So that spiritual barrenness continued on into your twenties?
Yeah. And yet that sense of destiny about what I was doing in terms of singing—that was definitely a dream that had been placed into me. I never lost the sense that that was what I was supposed to be doing. In *Chariots of Fire* one of guys says that when he runs he feels like God is smiling. I used to have that feeling, and I still do, when I'm singing. I feel like God is smiling, like this is what I'm supposed to be doing. That never left me.

But as I went on and did the big shows like *Cats*, *Les Mis* and *Phantom of the Opera*, my profile became very high. I had all the worldly things, the trappings of status and success, but I used to lie awake at three o'clock in the morning just feeling empty.

At what point did you decide to do something about this emptiness?
I met this lovely man called Peter Lowrey, who was my boyfriend for quite a few years, and he asked me to marry him. We didn't want to get married in a church because my last experience of church hadn't been very good and I thought it would be rather hypocritical. But yet, I really wanted it to be a Christian ceremony; just going back to my childhood roots of faith.

By a series of odd circumstances, we fell into the hands of a pastor called David Wraight. David is now the CEO of Youth for Christ International, but then he was the CEO of Youth for Christ Australia. A wonderful, wonderful man. He just walked with us and did premarital counselling with us. I remember saying to him at one stage, 'Look, I want to make it clear that I am not a born again Christian and I don't particularly like them.' And he said, 'Yes, well, I am.' And I thought, oops! But he was so un-offended. He ended up becoming a great friend and mentor and just stayed involved in our lives. And there was something about him and his wife and kids that was really attractive and irresistible. We felt drawn to them, and whenever we were going through any type of crisis or problem we always went to David.

One particular time we were dealing with some issues and David asked if we'd like him to pray for the situation. I remember Peter and I nervously looked at each other and said, 'OK, as long as it's not weird.' He prayed and it was just the most powerful moment. I felt like I had built up a sort of wall around my heart and I felt like it just crashed down when he prayed. I just wept and said, 'Oh, I need God back in my life.'

What happened for Peter?
I think he was kind of alarmed to see his wife go through this. But

being the lovely, accommodating person that he is, when I said that I really wanted to go to church Peter agreed. Actually, from the moment we had been married by David, Peter had been saying that we should go to church. 'I don't know why,' he'd say, 'I think it'd be good to go to church.' So that following Sunday we walked into a local little church and were welcomed and it was just a wonderful experience. And it was like the missing piece that had kept me awake at three o'clock in the morning was suddenly filled.

What a beautiful story. And that has taken you on to endorse some of the wonderful things being done by Christians around the world. You're the ambassador for the Operation Christmas Child project run by Samaritan's Purse, which sees gift-packed shoeboxes sent to children in developing countries.

I am, and that has been one of the greatest blessings in my life. I'm so honoured to be associated with these people. I've visited Cambodia twice to see the boxes being handed out, and my husband has been three times.

You have to remember that Cambodia underwent the Pol Pot regime where basically half of the population, over two million people, were killed. Consequently, there are orphans who have had children, who have then become orphans. There is a complete breakdown of infrastructure. There are kids working as sex workers from the age of six and seven. Kids are sent out to beg—there are begging rings. They live on garbage dumps. They live in places you wouldn't even put a dog into in this country.

To be able to just give these kids a gift and to actually esteem them and honour them is something that they have never experienced. It is like a little piece of heaven on earth for that moment.

The attention that is focused on you on the stage you can usher onto projects like Operation Christmas Child, which is a great opportunity to have.
In the past I have wondered why I have a platform. I mean, I love singing and all of that. But being able to use that to actually make people aware of Samaritan's Purse makes wonderful sense of my life.

Do you have any advice for the Christian wanting to follow in your footsteps and enter the arts world, while staying on the straight and narrow?
Christians are called to be salt and light. I love being a Christian where I work. Generally I'll be the only Christian in the cast, and while I hold very strongly to my beliefs, the people that I work with can see that I'm fun and that I relate. And by about day two of rehearsals we generally get into deep spiritual discussions. I love where I've been placed and I love being able to have an impact on people, just by my relationship with them. If you really feel that you are called to do something then do it. You can have some wonderful experiences.

And feel God smile.
Absolutely. It's a beautiful feeling.

Thomas Keneally

Thomas Keneally is one of Australia's most highly acclaimed writers. The author of nearly fifty works of fiction, non-fiction, memoir and screenplay, his work has been recognised with numerous literary honours, including a Booker Prize and two Miles Franklin awards. Best known for *Schindler's Ark*, the basis of the award-winning film *Schindler's List*, Tom Keneally joined us one night to talk about his play *Either Or*, which had just been touring the United States.

Kurt Gerstein, the central character of Either Or, *has been described by the Washington Times as 'The nicest Nazi in the slaughter house'. Is he a fictional character or did he actually exist during World War II?*
He existed. He was an evangelical Christian, which was not the style of his family at all. They considered him unduly religious. His sister-in-law to whom he had a strong relationship was gassed by the SS in 1940. There were a series of eugenic gassings of people who weren't perfect, like children with Down's Syndrome and people with various mental diseases. It is heartbreaking to think of. And his sister-in-law had a mental illness.

As a result of her being gassed, Gerstein joined the SS with the determined purpose to leaven the lump and bear witness. He saved a lot of lives by using a particular fumigant called Zyclon B to clean the uniforms and to fumigate the barracks of Russian prisoners of war. But after about a year he found himself invited to participate in the use of Zyclon B to actually gas warm-blooded animals—namely us, his fellow humans. To pay him credit, he almost immediately broke the news to the Allies, to various neutral nations and to the Papal Nuncio—the Vatican's ambassador—in Germany. Despite all this whistle-blowing, the response he got from the outside world left him in considerable despair.

At the end of the war he gave testimony against the killing machine, and then he was found hanged in his cell. Some people think he did it himself. I think it was done by his fellow SS men. He is characteristic of a man with an impossible moral dilemma who is not allowed to choose between absolute good and absolute evil, but finds himself in the situation where he has to choose, does so, and then tries to redeem himself by being the whistle-blower.

It is quite a storyline. You have this knack of finding such stories. How did you discover Kurt Gerstein?
I came across him while I was researching *Schindler*. In conventional terms Kurt Gerstein is not a sinner at all; he was a very moral character, a very powerful character, because I think a lot of us find now that a lot of decent human beings are put in a situation where they can't choose between absolute good and absolute evil. They can only try to work within the situation imposed on them, to do the least damage possible. Being a ruined seminarian from a Catholic seminary, these moral questions have always fascinated me. I partly wrote the Gerstein story to ask myself if I would be as brave as him in that extreme situation.

There's a story behind how you came across the character of Oscar Schindler as well.

I met a Jewish survivor in Beverly Hills, California, of all places, in 1980, when most of your listeners may not even have been born. I bought a briefcase in a store whose owner was a Jewish survivor of the Holocaust. He was a very impressive character in his own right. His name was Leopold; he was Polish. But he and his wife had been in Schindler's camp.

Even though I'm a ruined Catholic seminarian, I think there are wonderful texts in the Scriptures that explain Schindler. One of them is, 'The Spirit breatheth where he will.' The Spirit—it, he, whatever—doesn't always work through perfect channels. Schindler was certainly a highly imperfect channel. He was a black marketeer, he was an unsatisfactory husband, he was not as moral a man as Kurt Gerstein was. Yet it was through him that a certain ration of people, from the whole calamity of the Holocaust, was saved. That fascinates me, because writers are always interested in the paradox of the scoundrel saviour, the redeeming sinner. Since my childhood I have always been interested in such characters. Literature has always been interested in them.

Oscar was an extraordinary case of a businessman on whose premises no Jewish prisoner died of unnatural causes—unnatural causes being starvation, execution, sabotage or brutalisation by the SS. It seems to me that one of the problems that Western civilisation has to get over, one of the tests that we have always failed, is our relationship with our fellow members of the species Homo sapiens sapiens who happen to be Jewish.

Thomas, how was your emotional state as you wrote Schindler's Ark? *It deals with such a troubled time in history. The Holocaust was so horrific. How did you feel during the research process and during its writing?*

I live in an area of Sydney that I hope your listeners either know or will one day visit—the Northern Beaches. Even in this sunny environment, with all the board riders off Bilgola Beach where I live, I found that . . . You know, we writers like to think that we can go in, plunder a story and get out cheap. We grab the story but the story also grabs us. So I suffered a sort of, I suppose you could call it a depression about myself and about the human species, about half way through the writing. I still remember that—from about Spring of 1981. You don't get out with a clean skin at all.

Writers sometimes adopt superior moral airs and say, 'I like to write about ethnic hatred because it's so terrible.' And it is terrible. But also it's where the drama is. It's always where the good stories are. Just imagine the drama now in, say, Sydney, of a relationship between a descendant of western Europeans and a Muslim. Just imagine the tensions that generates. Love and fraternity across the lines of racist cultures and religions, that's always very interesting. And it is astonishing how many times individual people find a way through those minefields. I think in doing so they are following the call to love, which is at the core of the Christianity in which I was raised as a kid.

Let's turn to that then. You mentioned you were a 'ruined seminarian' . . .
Oh yes, indeed. I studied for the priesthood in the days when there was a lot of sectarianism in Australia, forgotten by most young Australians now. There was a certain mistrust of the Irish Catholics and so there were always a number of kids in every school who studied for the priesthood. I studied for the priesthood but I found it very tough. I found not just the celibacy tough; I found the biggest tension between our individual reason and our obedience. And that has always been the big crisis for Christians, hasn't it?

What did you find most difficult to pull together? What was the central issue that you were struggling with?

Well, look, I found that the big Christian institutions run the danger of becoming like any big institution, whether it be the Red Cross or an insurance company or whatever. The great problem is that sometimes they will write people off whom they consider to have failed them. That is something that I found very difficult to deal with. Some of my fellow students would either catch tuberculosis (and this was in Sydney in the 1950s), or would become psychiatric cases under the stress of pursuing their vocation. And when these things happened, the church withdrew and left it all to the family. I felt then, and I still do, that the church has a responsibility to look after its own.

Absolutely.

If it can't look after its own, who is it going to look after? So that knowledge was a big crisis for me, personally.

Then the other great problem was of democracy. We all have the right to believe what we will believe, but then there is the phenomenon of religious leaders in a number of groups saying, 'Those who are not with us are amongst the unenlightened and may even be amongst the damned.' Well, in a liberal democracy where everyone has the vote and everyone has human rights, who can say, without direct divine revelation, that anyone is damned? So there is an inevitable tension between democracy with its many groups, its many races, its many religions, and some doctrine you encounter which says, 'If you do not believe this set of beliefs and if you do not go through this set of observances you are amongst the damned.' That's the way I think about it anyhow.

Thomas, I'm really interested. What kind of picture or image of God were you brought up with, in your seminary days in particular?

Well, it was male. It was rather Aryan, rather white Anglo-Saxon or Anglo-Celtic. But like Kurt Gerstein says in the play, sometimes it's as if the God of the nice little churches withdraws and you are left with God the unutterable, God the unspeakable, God the indefinable, and I think it is quite possible that God evades all the nets of our definitions. Everything ineffable, whether it be love—whether romantic love or love for children—or whether it be an appreciation of the deity . . . there is something about our limited web of words. God knows I love words and live by them, but there are some realities that slip through our web of words. Whatever God is, I don't think it is reduced to the Y and the X chromosome which defines who we are.

Is there anything of that Christian past that you still retain? What are your feelings on the person of Jesus these days?

That's interesting because I increasingly examine Christ, and what I find is that there is a model for life there. If we can abstract from the question of divinity for a moment . . . There is no question that he thought he was the Son of God, but let's abstract from that if you will permit me for a moment.

There are wonderful enduring aphorisms such as, 'Don't get yourself all in a lather, your Father knows if one sparrow falls from heaven.' 'If you would be my disciple, give all you have to the poor and come follow me.' There are many texts that I find, as I get to be an old inheritor of the King James Bible, that I find very comforting. And of course above all there is that great statement of St Paul, that you can do everything—win an Aussie Rules or Rugby League grand final, win gold medals, whatever—but if you have not love you are as 'sounding brass and tinkling cymbals'. I still follow the proposition in my daily life that if you 'do this to the least of my brethren you do it to me'. Sometimes you look at politicians and you wonder how they can hear that read aloud in the churches they attend and still pursue some of the policies they do.

As you speak I think of a chat I had with the cartoonist Michael Leunig some time ago. He was saying how, as he got older, he was reflecting more and more on the person of Jesus. I wonder, Thomas, whether the qualities that Jesus possesses and the love and the messages that still continue to resound from him—I wonder if they would have been possible if he weren't *divine.*
Yes, well, that's one of 'the proofs'. Yes, indeed. I take that on board . . .

I'm baiting you, you know.
Yes, indeed. Ah, but it's good to bait old buggers like me!

Why are you a novelist, Thomas? In the end, why have you chosen this particular profession as your career, as your calling?
I still think of it, rightly or wrongly, as the biggest game for the human species to play. The business of trying to tell a story, of trying to bring the elements together, to create an engaging, an engrossing, an enlightening tale . . . It's partly ego, there is no denying that. But there have always been people who wanted to tell stories around the campsite. It's one of our ancient descriptions; we are a species that tells stories.

From the time when I was a kid I was very impressed with the priesthood, the mystery of the priesthood, the sacraments and all the rest of it. But I also thought there is this great bag of tricks that the novelist has, and I would love to try to deploy them. I had no idea how difficult it was, and I had no idea that at seventy-one I'd still be struggling towards producing a good final story on the back of which I could then say, '*Nunc dimittis*: Lord, now lettest thou thy servant depart in peace.'

I had a friend named Morris West who lived near me and died in his eighties at the end of a very good paragraph. He was still struggling to write the good book, and I think I will be doing that till the end of my days. A lifetime is barely enough for the task that we face and all the possibilities of the human soul.

Thomas, listening to you speak, a thought comes to mind about the connection with the priesthood and your vocation as a writer. I wonder if the central intersection point of the two is 'meaning'. It seems to me that the great novelists, the great fiction writers, are in many ways exploring the great themes of meaning in life.

Oh yes, there is no question that there is a similarity between where I began and where I've ended up. I would not even want to deny that it is so. Meaning is everything and humans will never cease pursuing the question of meaning. Nor should they. Indeed, nor can they. We're almost hard-wired to pursue the questions of meaning and significance. There is no escaping it, wherever you go.

Graham Kendrick

He's written some of the most widely sung contemporary Christian songs of our time: 'Amazing Love', 'The Servant King', 'Shine Jesus Shine'. Described as a father of modern worship music, Graham Kendrick was also one of the founders of the global phenomenon called *March for Jesus* which mobilised millions of Christians to bring praise, prayer and acts of goodwill to the streets of their cities.

For Kendrick, worship of God incorporates not just music but mercy, not just poetry but justice. Through his thirty-plus albums and hundreds of songs, he encourages us to understand worship as a way of life, and true intimacy with God as sharing in the concerns of God's heart and participating in his mission to the world.

You've released thirty-odd albums and written hundreds of songs, yet I believe your very first music teacher gave up on you.
I had some piano lessons when I was quite young; I think it was probably too soon. Just the other day, in fact, I came across this notebook among my father's stuff—homework after music lessons. I came across one comment from the music teacher about me, where she said, 'You're wasting my time'!

[Laughter]

243

Possibly it was almost a provocation that some years later I picked up the guitar and thought, 'Right, I'm going to get some sounds out of this all by myself.' It sort of set me off experimenting, which is I guess what song writing is all about. It's about finding fresh sounds that inspire you.

Very early on you and a few others jumped into a minivan and began to travel and sing without any planned means of financial support. Tell me about that.

In my early twenties some of us got together, very keen to share our faith and wanting to work with local churches. We were all young, we wanted to connect with young people and we felt we had the skills to do that, so off we went. We were very idealistic, and, you know, had we known the problems we might not even have started. But this is the great thing about being young and naïve, isn't it? You just do it, and we did, and we survived.

I had a very clear idea of myself as a kind of performer doing concerts, and that was what I thought I would do on this team. As it turned out, I spent a lot of time just sitting around talking to people, discussing the Christian faith, and leading singing in churches, which I hadn't really done much of—not knowing that that would actually become a very large part of my life.

Tell me about that transition from performance to leading worship— leading singing and other expressions of devotion to God.

In my twenties there was a whole new wave of renewal happening in the churches. It really hit worship and I got caught up with that. Previously church worship was fairly formal and based around hymn singing and the pastor leading everything. But then people started to experience God a lot more in public worship—

there was an expectation that you would actually feel God was there, and the meeting would be shaped by this sense of God's presence. And new songs started being written which were an awful lot more personal. They would address God directly; you would speak *to* God in the songs. I don't think we realised at the time, but something was starting which would eventually work right through and become mainstream—which I think is now the case.

Worship has become much more contemporary in style, and I think, on the whole, that has been a good thing. In history, in every generation where there has been an experience of God and a sense of God doing new things, it's come out in new music.

That's very true. You would've reflected on this word 'worship'. How would you define it now, and what has been the real thrust and focus of it for you personally?
I think it's true to say that everybody worships something. Anthropologists who study different cultures will say there is one thing that is consistent with every kind of culture, whether it's primitive or sophisticated—everywhere there is worship.

Obviously what is worshipped varies incredibly, but there is something about just being human which means that we naturally look beyond ourselves. I would say that's because that's how we were made. There is a God who created us and our highest purpose is to know that God and to be in relationship with that God. So I think for me the word worship implies relationship—knowing God. And of course, this is what the Christian faith is all about. It is God reaching to mankind in a very tangible way through Jesus Christ, the Son of God, God made flesh. There's a whole lot wrapped up in those few words, but it's basically God coming to us and saying, 'Here is a way that you can be reconciled to me and have relationship.'

Jesus talked of God as 'Father', which in his day was quite radical. He said that the Father is seeking worshippers. So to worship in the Christian sense is all about finding God in a way that he can be known and experienced, having peace with God, and peace with one another as well. Out of that flows things like songs. Worship is not singing, but singing is a great way to express worship.

When I first became a Christian one of the first songs of yours that I heard was 'Shine Jesus Shine'. It probably remains the best known Graham Kendrick song in Australia. Is there a story behind it at all?
There is no great dramatic story behind it. But at the time I was very caught up with this whole sense of how we approach God. You know, God is a holy God and we are sinful people, so there was a theme woven in there of being able to approach God through what Jesus did by his death on the cross. And I think the journey of the song then takes us outwards to a prayer for the nations to know this God and to experience the love that comes from God on a bigger scale.

The song itself actually came in two parts. I wrote the verses separately, envisioning them originally as a song in themselves. I tried them out in my local church in London at the time and it was just an OK song, such that I put it away. I looked at it again a few months later. I think there was an event coming up where I was asked to submit some songs, and I sang these verses to myself again and thought, 'These are verses, and I need a chorus.' And very quickly the ideas came to mind. It dropped together in an unusually fast way.

How do you write your music? Does the inspiration suddenly come, or is it more a case of continuing to write and rewrite a song?
I'm probably more the write and rewrite guy. But you have to have those moments of inspiration—something which, although it might be in the midst of hard work, sort of touches you in some way, moves and stirs you, such that you think there is a song in here just waiting to get out.

I am very spontaneous in certain situations, but it won't necessarily produce a song. For example, one thing I do a lot of these days is what I call 'Psalm surfing' where with a bunch of people I open up a Psalm and just start to extemporise a tune around it and have people join in. I just sing a line and they sing after me, and it's kind of a linear journey through a Psalm. Occasionally something will stick that I'll think might be the basis of a song, but mostly it's just for that moment.

One of the songs on the new album *Out of the Ordinary*, called 'Crucified Man', I distinctly remember beginning about eight years ago. Back then it just didn't make it, so I put it aside, and then about two years ago I looked at it again, rewrote it and it finally came together.

You were also one of the founders of the March for Jesus *movement, which started in London with people hitting the streets publicly declaring their faith in Jesus. It later spread to other countries; 177 countries and twelve 12 million people or something were actually involved in it at one point.*
Yes. I can remember doing it around Canberra actually, and Adelaide. It was in 1994—the first year it went global. I flew down to New Zealand on that occasion and took part in the first march and then crossed the dateline and took part in the last march in

about twenty-four hours, which was quite an experience.

That was definitely one of those phenomena that you could not have planned. I had this feeling that we needed to take some of the fresh life and joy that was happening inside our church buildings and take it out onto the streets. I began to write some music for that, because we needed a form, a shape, to it and it became a sort of musical procession. I called it a praise march. To my amazement it suddenly took off. This was the mid-1980s and all across the UK churches of all different denominations started to unite and do this. We had some phenomenal gatherings. In London we had about 55,000 people gathered, and about a quarter of a million people across the country in separate marches. One year it went Europe-wide, then global, and it finally finished in the year 2000.

Some of the marches continue in some places. Have we lost something now that we don't have that kind of public gathering? Or do you think the season came and went?
Yeah. I think one of the problems is when we try and perpetuate something that has had its day. We didn't call an end to it; I think the message we put out was, 'It's not "over", it's "over to you".' We said to people, 'Look, we're not going to coordinate this globally anymore, but if you see a need for it in your city, then go for it.' In fact, down in Sao Paulo, Brazil, they have up to two million people come out for a March for Jesus every year. So there is quite a heritage there.

But other things take their place, and I think you have to make space for new things. In the UK there have been events like The Message and Soul in the City where the next generation have come out on the streets. But it's been a slightly different expression which is more appropriate in the current day.

Well, you have a letter from your first music teacher saying 'stop wasting my time', yet you've been used by God to co-found movements like March for Jesus *and the big UK event* Spring Harvest. *You've written hundreds of worship songs, many of them sung right around the world. You've been used in an area that originally you weren't expecting. Reflecting on your life so far, what have you learned about God's guidance, leading and calling through these experiences?*

I think that everybody does potentially have a particular pathway for them to go on. It's like an offer, I think. If you put your life in God's hands then that's exactly what it means—it's no longer your life; it's in God's hands to do with what he wants. As a child I always had a sense that there was something for me to do. I didn't know what it was; it just shaped up step by step, year by year.

But I think it boils down to trying to offer up every day to God, serving him in whatever way. We love to have our big plans, things which make us feel significant in the world, but I think the danger there is that we just try to live in the future. Things don't actually exist yet. But I think each day it's important to say, 'God, what have you got for me to do? However humble it is, I will do it.' Then I think God does the rest. He guides and directs us, and it's not always according to our own preconceived ideas of what we can or can't do, or what we're good at. God generally does know best, which shouldn't be a surprising thing. But sometimes we don't trust him.

So I've tried to live my life with that sense of, 'God, what have you got for me to do? I'm basically your servant.' My experience is that God has been faithful to that; I've always had something to do which I sense has been valuable and worthwhile.

You've been leading people in worship all these years. What's the one characteristic of God, that one characteristic of Jesus, that you're most enamoured of?

I think it's what we call grace, which basically means undeserved favour. God doesn't owe us anything at all but he chooses, because he loves us, to pour favour upon us. Our job is simply to choose whether or not we receive that favour. It's not automatic; it requires a response of faith that we then trust God with our lives.

Definitely, the more I go on, the more I'm just in awe of this thing that we call grace and I'm more and more thankful for it. It's something which evokes and draws worship out of me. Worship is a response, and when you look at God's grace, what can you do but just respond and say, 'Wow! Thank you.'

Adrian Plass

BACON SANDWICHES AND SALVATION

Adrian Plass is a British writer, speaker and humorist. In the last twenty years he has produced over thirty books of fiction, biography and poetry, with his best-known book, *The Sacred Diary of Adrian Plass (Age 37¾)*, selling hundreds of thousands of copies worldwide.

A 'bemused Anglican', Adrian's trademark wit, satire and storytelling revolve largely around his own inadequacies as a Christian. When he joined us on Open House we talked about God, humour, the breakdown that started his writing career . . . and bacon sandwiches. On seeking Adrian's permission to include his interview in this book I received the following reply: 'Go ahead and use the interview. My only stipulation is that if I said anything sacrilegious you print it in capital letters.'

You've been warned.

Adrian, the last time you and I spoke we were in a radio station in Perth. You were a little late to the interview, but we forgave you for that.
Very good of you, but you are lumbered when you're a Christian, aren't you?

Well, yes, I had to forgive you! At one stage during the interview I said, 'Adrian, what does God laugh at?' You paused for a moment, looked me straight in the eye, and said—'You'.
[Laughter]
Well, I mean, it's a pretty safe bet.

Oh, thank you.
Anybody who claims to be a Christian is probably going to be smiled at, at the very least, by God occasionally, because we are the most ludicrous creatures. I certainly have the odd admirable sane moments, but I mean, when you travel as much as I do and you hear what people say and the claims they make and the appalling certainty they have about some things, I can't help feeling that more often than we might think God says, 'Oh yeah, yeah, yeah,' and just waits for us to come to our senses. He probably laughs and cries in equal measure.

Well, if he laughs at me, what does he do at you?
Oh, he thinks I'm utterly ridiculous, I'm quite sure. I remember a time and . . . people talk about God talking to them, I'm not saying that, but I was walking along one day heading for a meeting and feeling wretched—you know, really inadequate. I had a row with my wife or something; I can't remember what it was. And I remember saying to God in my mind, 'I can't do this. I cannot go and stand up and pretend to represent you in some miserable way when I am actually a rat.' And if he said anything to me in reply, I think the atmosphere of it was, 'You go sit in a corner, tear yourself to pieces, feel sorry for yourself, beat yourself to death, but don't ever despise what I do through you.' I think that is the point in the end.

You've just written a book called Bacon Sandwiches and Salvation. *You have got to be the first person in the world to draw the previously unknown link between the two.*
Well, the link seems so obvious to me that I'm amazed anyone even questions it.

[Laughter]

In our church there is a lady called Liz Pearce who is a wonderful, generous, giving person, but all her life she has been a magistrate and a schools inspector. So she has a lifetime of flippancy stored up in her that was never given a vent and which means in church she is very naughty. I was sitting at the back of the church with her one day and the minister said, 'What's the most important thing in the world?' I for once rather piously said 'salvation', and she said 'bacon sandwiches'. And I thought, '*That's right*: the God who can create salvation *and* bacon sandwiches must be worth following.'

It's only a step from there to imagine bacon ministry where you speak to thousands of people and you fry bacon up the front and you say, 'If anyone wants to make a commitment to Christ they can have a bacon sandwich, but if not they don't get one.' They would flood to the front.

So that's the origin of the title, and it's really just an alphabetical glossary of Christian terms with my rather individualist interpretations attached.

Give us an example then. What kind of Christian terms do you explore in the book?
Well, there are so many. 'Bless you', for instance, actually means 'clear off'.

[Laughter]

'A' for 'Astrology' is an interesting one: 'The study of the movement of relative positions of celestial bodies interpreted as an influence on human affairs.' And of course as Christians we just thank our lucky stars that we don't have to get involved with that.

Boom, tish!
'Born Again Christians'—that really means 'bigoted, narrow-minded gits'. Well, of course it doesn't, but I don't know if it's the same in Australia, but in Britain we have somehow managed to distort and dissolve that phrase—which is an essential Christian belief—and make it mean exactly that.

I was speaking to a secular interviewer on radio and he said, 'You're not one of them born again Christians, are you?' I said, 'Well, what's the other sort then?' He said, 'You know what I mean.' And I said, 'Yeah, you mean am I a bigoted narrowed-minded git?' And he said, 'Well, I suppose that is what I mean.' What a terrible, terrible thing to have done.

Oh, one more: 'Christian Bookshops'—'Places offering a wide range of narrow literature, usually called something with *Vine* in it. Hence *The Vine, The Fruit of the Vine, Vine Leaves, Vine Branch, Vine Harvest, Grape Vine, Off the Vine, On the Vine, Up the Vine, Down the Vine, Round the Vine, Cut Round the Back of the Vine, Pluck from the Vine, Drop from the Vine, Root of the Vine, Wine from the Vine*, etc., etc.'

[Laughter]

Well if you haven't pieced this together already, we're talking to Adrian Plass. He's an author and . . . I want to say 'comedian', but do you like the word 'humorist' better?
I have always avoided the term comedian because I never was one.

I began years ago when I had a dreadful illness and I wrote *The Sacred Diary*, which really came out of a lot of frustration and anger and worry about whether the whole thing of church and faith was just a load of rubbish. I was very serious then and I am very serious now, and although I do use humour as a vehicle, I am a very angsty, passionate person really, about what I believe and what I think. I wrote a book a little while ago called *Jesus: Safe, Tender, Extreme* which is a kind of rounding up my feelings about the faith to date, and that was a fairly serious book. So this present book is a cathartic release from the intensity of that. But still I can't help it—it still makes mysterious points.

Your early profession was looking after children in need, and you also have a theatre background as well. There are a number of things flowing through your veins.

I am a very lucky person, you know. If someone had got a committee together to decide how Adrian should live, what I am doing is what they would've come up with. It's fantastic. I do a bit of acting, quite a bit of speaking, writing of course, and I travel a lot and meet lots of people to talk endlessly with and chew on lots of ideas. I just love it all. I don't mean that I don't get depressed because I do. But I love my job, and it's just wonderful considering what it came out of, which was abject failure.

Let's touch on that. It was 1984 and you had something of a breakdown. What led to it? What were the main causes of that kind of disillusion for you?

As far as I can tell there were three, maybe four things. One was just my general fragility. I wasn't a very real person and I kind of cobbled together a personality that worked but it wasn't very solid.

It only needed a little kick at the bottom for the whole thing to come down.

The other was the church, which was driving me bonkers. I really wanted it all to be right and true, but there was so much kind of benevolent hypocrisy where we say one thing and do another, or we say we believe one thing and it doesn't work and we produce a list of reasons why it does. So all that stuff.

I guess, thirdly, I was working with really difficult children. Although I loved the children, I was working in a secure assessment unit with very violent children and kids who were likely to abscond. There was just nowhere to send them, and some of these were great kids. So if you take all of that and put it in a bag, it was just too much and I abdicated from responsibility for a while, and that was the centre of the crack-up really.

How long were you in those deep valleys of despair? How long did it take for you to come out and laugh again?
Relatively, not very long—I guess about a year. I always had very good support from my family and also from one or two friends who didn't quote Scripture verses to me and didn't offer me ministry except in the best and purest form, which is having a pint in the pub with you and just being with you. And writing was the great therapy. I'd never really done it before and I used to sit in my upstairs sitting room struggling away and wondering if anyone would ever be interested in what I was writing. But it was more than that, because it took all this dirty water off my chest.

The Sacred Diary of Adrian Plass *catapulted you into the Christian publishing stratosphere. In it you really poked fun at the church, obviously as a result of some of the experiences you had. Were you ever fearful of treading on 'sacred ground'?*

Well, one of the advantages of being in a stress illness and coming out of it is you don't give a tinkers about what anybody else thinks. That is one of the major problems for Christian artists and writers, I think, that there is such a weight of worry about what people are going to think. I was in the unusual position of simply writing from the heart because I didn't care. So I was writing the truth about how I felt. *The Sacred Diary* could've been a very serious, bitter, angry book. My wife said, 'You know no one's going to read it if it's like that, don't you?' So I made it funny and it poured out. I think when people read it they were just amazed to find they were not alone, and I was amazed to find that I was not alone; that a lot of these peripheral activities—the arm raising and the silly things, you know—are not that important.

In this book there's something about 'Fraudulent Teaching' and the definition of it is: 'The teaching that says you can't do it, only God can do it. But then when you find you can't do it says it's your fault.' That's one of the little prisons that people often find themselves in. It was just wonderful to burst out of all that.

In your writings you've made a lot of us adults becoming like children. In one of your books you describe a big businessman, obviously with a bit of weight, who loiters round a bouncy castle. You talk about him being this 'big blob of congealed dignity', which I think is a beautiful phrase. Finally he climbs onto the bouncy castle and has a play. That whole concept of adults becoming like kids again, where does that spring from?

Well, from the Bible really. All the best things seem to come from the things Jesus said, and Jesus said, 'Unless you become like a little child you cannot enter the kingdom of God.'

But it's also come from dealing with my own life and my own past. I don't know whether this is true for you and for the listeners, but sometimes you have to go back to the kid inside you and sort a few things out. I think I had to find the child in me again, or allow the child to play and be a happy child of God—not a miserable, troubled servant of God. We *are* servants, but we are also children of God, and discovering that again is such a relief.

You know, people don't seem to like God very much. They respect him; they say he is awesome and all this other stuff. But one of the key things that helped me when I was recovering was simply pedalling a bike round and round. I felt as though, absurd though it sounds, that God was sitting on the back door step while I was just cycling round. It's the purest form of prayer that I can think of. You are just with him. When you know you are loved—and I think the first task of the Christian is to be loved—you can start to be obedient because you are truly motivated. I think an awful lot of churches and books and teaching start from the point of fear and obligation, and I don't know that that works with very many people.

Adrian, what I like about talking with you is that you can be funny and you can be serious. There is a depth to you, not just some surface-level personality. But do you ever feel pressured to be funny?
Yes, I do. I sometimes find it very heavy. I occasionally go to dinners to speak, and the time eating before I speak I sometimes find quite difficult because I can see people looking at me and thinking, 'How is this morose individual ever going to stand up and do anything funny?' Sometimes the pressure to be a clown is a little oppressive, because I'm definitely not that.

What advice would you give to the person aspiring to write; to write satirical work or write novels, or to be involved in the arts in some way?
Well, certainly go with your passion. All the best things I have ever written came out of passion. By that I don't just mean passion about faith; I mean passion about tress, birds, sky, trains, travelling—anything. Where you feel passion stirring within you there will be something there to write about. I know that sounds obvious but it's such a natural pathway for creativity.

If you're a Christian, remember that if you're not on the edge you're not really anywhere. When you read the gospels, when you read the history of the heroes of the Christian faith, they are always on the edge. You will always be juggling what is acceptable and what isn't, and what is indulgent on your part and what is truly useful, and you're going to end up upsetting a few people and hopefully helping many more.

For humour all I would say is you have to do it from inside, not from outside. You've got to love the church to be usefully humorous about it. You've got to love all us silly, foolish, loveable, strangely shaped people. When you laugh at the church don't laugh at individual people, but laugh at us the way *we* are.

Adrian, as we leave I want to say there is no pressure to be funny right now, OK?
Oh, right, yeah.

[Open House producer] Kirsty and I thought it might be a little bit of fun to end on a word association game. We thought, if we throw a few words and phrases at Adrian Plass, who knows what might come out?
You want me to respond with individual words or thoughts?

Words, thoughts or stories. Really, whatever comes into your mind. OK, first word: Anglicans.

[Laughter]

Well, I have tried to define Anglicans in my book and because we're such a broad church now it's really, really difficult. I've defined them as 'those who approve of women in the priesthood and those who don't approve of women in the priesthood,' and I think one of the other ones is, 'an Anglican is someone who, when "Worthy is the Lamb" is being sung, turns to her neighbour and says, "I hope the joint's big enough".'

[Laughter]

Word number two: Australians.

When we toured Australia I wrote a little piece based on our travels, and the moment I remember best happened when I was in Queensland. I went into a chemist and asked for something for the mosquitoes, and this chap said [puts on broad Australian accent], 'Right, here's the stuff to stop the mozzies biting, and here's the stuff to put on after it hasn't worked.'

[Laughter]

I don't know if that sums up anything quintessentially Australian.

As a born and bred Queenslander, I can certainly identify with that. OK, number three: British people.

I think we have changed over the last couple of decades. We used to be very non-huggy people and [now] there is a kind of culture of shadow hugging going on. In the church it's a little bit worrying because you see men heading for the most attractive women in the room to give her a holy hug. I think perhaps we've let it go a little over the top; I think a little more discriminate hugging is called for. But I will tell you something, I just love England. Every year I'm alive I love it more. I think April, May and June in England is just about as heavenly as you get.

Your second last word: Journalists.
Well, there's a variable bunch. My immediate response is that I remember so many local radio interviews where the journalist hasn't read the book and is hastily reading stuff off the back cover and I realised within a very short time that I'm simply filling in a gap. Then I think of people like yourself, where you have an interview which really does speak to you and opens up all sorts of areas, and one of the great things about interviews like that is that you find yourself discovering things that you hadn't thought of before and kind of making notes.

As for written journalists, well, I try not to read things that are written about me any more because I think I'd agree with Kipling that praise and damnation are both impostors.

I don't know what you're going to do with this one, but here's the final word in our association game: God.
Well, I have a long list of questions for God when I get to heaven. My great fear is that he'll have an even longer list for me. I think he probably will. But the whole thought of God makes me laugh, makes me cry, makes me smile, and makes me angry. I just don't understand. In my heart I feel a well of . . . something . . . about God, and I yearn for the day when the whole thing's sorted out.

I sometimes really worry about God. There's a verse in Second Peter which says that God doesn't want anyone to be lost. Are we going to have a very disappointed God in that sense, if God can actually feel disappointment? I don't know. He isn't going to get what he wants.

We may be amazed at how warm and fatherly God is when we finally meet face to face. I don't know. But he's at the centre of my life anyway—everything I do and think and write.

About Sheridan Voysey

Sheridan Voysey is a Sydney-based writer, speaker and broadcaster.

Sheridan is the author of the award-winning *Unseen Footprints: Encountering the Divine Along the Journey of Life*, named the 2006 Christian Book of the Year by the Australian Christian Literature Society. He is a featured columnist for *Alive Magazine*, and has been published in a variety of national and international publications.

Sheridan speaks regularly on issues of contemporary life, faith and culture. Passionate about everyday people hearing the whispers of God and changing their world, Sheridan speaks across denominations and in mainstream settings.

As a broadcaster Sheridan hosts Open House, the live, national talk show on which the interviews in this book first aired. He spent three years as creative director for *Compassion Day*—a national radio event in partnership with Compassion Australia which sees hundreds of children released from poverty each year.

Sheridan is married to Merryn, loves Thai food, is somewhat partial to dark chocolate, devours books, values solitude, hopes to one day own a puppy and is constantly working on his sense of humour.

His website is www.thethoughtfactory.net

Join the conversation

openhouse

Open House is Australia's live, three-hour talkback radio show exploring life, faith and culture. Join Sheridan Voysey every Sunday night, 8.00–11.00 pm EST, for compelling interviews, engaging talkback, book, film and TV reviews, and expert opinion on the issues of the day. You'll hear inspiring stories of faith, grapple with the big questions of life, and catch the odd live music performance along the way.

To find a participating station near you, or to subscribe to the podcast, visit www.theopenhouse.net.au

There was a quality of grace and warmth in Sheridan's manner that I greatly appreciated, and that I've experienced on only a few other programs.

—Author, ChristianityTodayMovies.com columnist
Jeffrey Overstreet

. . . every show explores questions that I'm personally asking, while making me aware of issues I haven't previously considered . . . I wish it were daily!

—Author and speaker **Jason Stevens**

. . . informative, challenging, sometimes funny, sometimes sad, always enlightening.

—Actress **Lynne McGranger**, 'Irene Roberts' on *Home and Away*

Open House is a production of Sydney's 1032: www.fm1032.com.au